G000123115

Tunisia: Understanding Successful Socioeconomic Development

A Joint World Bank–Islamic Development Bank Evaluation of Assistance

2005
The World Bank
Washington, D.C.

Islamic Development Bank
Jeddah, Saudi Arabia

http://www.worldbank.org/oed
http://www.isdb.org

ISBN 0-8213-5974-6
e-ISBN 0-8213-5975-4

Library of Congress Cataloging-in-Publication data have been applied for.

World Bank InfoShop
E-mail: pic@worldbank.org
Telephone: 202-458-5454
Facsimile: 202-522-1500

Operations Evaluation Department
Knowledge Programs and Evaluation Capacity
Development (OEDKE)
E-mail: eline@worldbank.org
Telephone: 202-458-4497
Facsimile: 202-522-3125

 Printed on Recycled Paper

Contents

Acknowledgments

Fareed M. A. Hassan was the Task Manager for this report and acknowledges with thanks the contributions by Adil Kanaan, Elaine W. Ooi, and Isabelle Tsakok (consultants). Ibrahim A. Elbadawi and Jorge Garcia-Garcia reviewed the report. Gonzalo Salinas provided statistical information, and Janice Joshi, administrative support.

The evaluation is the second cooperative effort with the Islamic Development Bank, following the joint evaluation of the Jordan program. The support of Bader Eddine Nouioua, Adviser, Operations Evaluation and Audit, IDB, and Djelloul Al-Saci, Head, Operations Evaluation Office, IDB, is greatly acknowledged. Gregory K. Ingram, Director-General, Operations Evaluation; Ajay Chhibber, Director, Operations Evaluation Department; and Kyle Peters, Senior Manager, OEDCR, provided overall guidance, with substantial input into the formulation of the report.

Special thanks are due to the officials of the government of Tunisia for their valuable assistance and to the civil society and donor representatives interviewed in the country. The report has also benefited significantly from helpful and constructive suggestions from numerous World Bank, IDB, and IMF staff.

Director-General, Operations Evaluation:
Gregory K. Ingram
Director, Operations Evaluation Department:
Ajay Chhibber
Senior Manager, Country Evaluation &
Regional Relations: *R. Kyle Peters*
Task Manager: *Fareed M.A. Hassan*

PREFACE

ENGLISH

This Country Assistance Evaluation (CAE) on Tunisia is the second cooperative effort with the Operations Evaluation Office (OEO) of the Islamic Development Bank, following the joint OED-OEO assessment of the Jordan Program. The two institutions carried out a joint assessment of Tunisia's economic and social development since 1990 and the challenges facing the country. There will be two separate reports; the assessments of each institution's assistance program were prepared in parallel. This report benefited from consultations and comments from OEO staff, and the two evaluations generally agree on their analysis. The Executive Summary of the Islamic Development Bank's report is attached (Attachment 1).

A joint OED-OEO mission visited Tunisia in September 2003. The visit was facilitated by arrangements made by the staff of the Tunisian Ministry of Economic Development and International Cooperation. Their cooperation and assistance is gratefully acknowledged.

The report is organized as follows: Chapter 1 assesses Tunisia's socioeconomic development and the challenges ahead. This chapter is common to the evaluation reports of both the World Bank and the Islamic Development Bank. The subsequent chapters examine the effectiveness of World Bank assistance in addressing these challenges. The last chapter presents recommendations.

This Country Assistance Evaluation was written by Fareed M.A.

PREFACIO

La presente Evaluación de la Asistencia al País (EAP) para Túnez es la segunda iniciativa en cooperación con la Oficina de Evaluación de Operaciones (OEO) del Banco Islámico de Desarrollo (BIsD), tras la evaluación conjunta del DEO y la OEO del Programa para Jordania. Ambas instituciones llevaron a cabo una evaluación conjunta del desarrollo económico y social de Túnez desde 1990, así como de los desafíos que el país enfrenta. Se entregarán dos informes independientes; las evaluaciones del programa de asistencia de cada institución han sido elaboradas en paralelo. Este informe contó con el aporte de consultas y comentarios del personal de la Oficina de Evaluación de Operaciones; en términos generales, las dos evaluaciones concuerdan en su análisis. Se adjunta la Reseña del informe del Banco Islámico de Desarrollo (Anexo 1).

En septiembre de 2003, una misión conjunta del DEO y la OEO efectuó una visita a Túnez. La visita fue propiciada por las gestiones del personal del Ministerio de Desarrollo Económico y Cooperación Internacional de Túnez, al que debemos nuestro reconocimiento y gratitud por su cooperación y asistencia.

El informe se organiza como se detalla a continuación. El Capítulo 1 evalúa el desarrollo socioeconómico de Túnez y los desafíos futuros. Ese capítulo es común a los informes de evaluación del Banco Mundial y el Banco Islámico de Desarrollo. Los capítulos subsiguientes examinan la

PRÉFACE

La présente Évaluation de l'aide par pays (CAE) sur la Tunisie est le second effort de collaboration avec le Bureau de l'évaluation des opérations (OEO) de la Banque islamique de développement, suite à l'évaluation conjointe OED-OEO du Programme jordanien. Les deux institutions ont mené à bien une évaluation conjointe du développement économique et social de la Tunisie depuis 1990 et des défis auxquels est confronté le pays. Il y aura deux rapports séparés ; l'évaluation du programme d'aide de chaque institution a été préparée en parallèle. Ce rapport a bénéficié des consultations et des commentaires du personnel de l'OEO et les deux évaluations concordent de manière générale dans leur analyse. La note de synthèse du rapport de la Banque islamique de développement est ci-jointe (Pièce jointe 1).

Une mission conjointe OED-OEO s'est rendue en Tunisie en septembre 2003. Cette visite a été facilitée par les arrangements effectués par le personnel du Ministère tunisien du développement économique et de la coopération internationale. Nous tenons ici à les remercier de leur coopération et de leur aide.

Le rapport est organisé comme suit : Le chapitre 1 est une évaluation du développement socioéconomique de la Tunisie et des défis auxquels elle va être confrontée. Ce chapitre est commun aux deux rapports d'évaluation, celui de la Banque mondiale et celui de la Banque islamique de développement. Dans les chapitres suivants

ENGLISH

Hassan (Task Manager) with contributions by Djelloul Al-Saci (IDB); Adil Kanaan, Isabelle Tsakok, and Elaine W. Ooi (Consultants). Gonzalo Salinas and Janice Joshi provided statistical analysis and administrative support.

Ibrahim Elbadawi and Jorge Garcia-Garcia peer-reviewed the report. The assistance of peer reviewers in providing detailed comments on an earlier draft is gratefully acknowledged. Those comments, as well as others, received during OED's management review meeting, have been taken into account in the evaluation.

Comments from the Regional Management of the Bank have also been reflected in the report. The Regional response to the Management Action Record is included as Annex D. Copies of the draft report were sent to the government for review, and no written comments were received.

ESPAÑOL

eficacia de la asistencia del Banco Mundial para abordar estos desafíos. El último capítulo presenta recomendaciones.

Esta Evaluación de Asistencia al País ha sido redactada por Fareed M.A. Hassan (Gerente de tareas), con los aportes de Djelloul Al-Saci (BIsD); Adil Kanaan, Isabelle Tsakok y Elaine W. Ooi (Consultores). Gonzalo Salinas y Janice Joshi brindaron análisis estadísticos y apoyo administrativo.

Ibrahim Elbadawi y Jorge Garcia-Garcia estuvieron a cargo de la revisión entre pares del informe. Deseamos destacar nuestro agradecimiento a los colegas revisores por la ayuda prestada. Sus comentarios detallados, así como otros recibidos durante la reunión de análisis de gestión, se han tenido en cuenta en la evaluación.

El informe también refleja las observaciones de los directivos de la Oficina Regional del Banco. Se incluye, como Anexo D, la respuesta regional al Registro de Acción de Gestión. Se han enviado al gobierno copias del informe preliminar para su análisis, y no se han recibido comentarios por escrito.

FRANÇAIS

est examinée l'efficacité de l'aide de la Banque mondiale dans la façon d'aborder ces défis. Dans le dernier chapitre sont faites des recommandations.

L'Évaluation de l'aide par pays a été rédigée par Fareed M.A. Hassan (Chef de projet) avec la contribution de Djelloul Al-Saci (BID), Adil Kanaan, Isabelle Tsakok et Elaine W. Ooi (Consultants). Gonzalo Salinas et Janice Joshi ont apporté les analyses statistiques et le soutien administratif.

Ibrahim Elbadawi et Jorge Garcia-Garcia ont été réviseurs-pairs pour ce rapport. Nous tenons à remercier les réviseurs-pairs pour avoir apporté leurs commentaires détaillés sur une version antérieure du document. Il a été tenu compte dans l'évaluation de ces commentaires, ainsi que d'autres commentaires reçus au cours de la réunion de réexamen de la direction de l'OED.

Il a également été tenu compte dans ce rapport des commentaires de la Direction régionale de la Banque. La réponse régionale aux résultats des mesures de gestion figure à l'Annexe D. Copie du projet de rapport a été adressé au Gouvernement pour examen et aucun commentaire écrit n'a été reçu.

EXECUTIVE SUMMARY

This Country Assistance Evaluation was prepared in collaboration with the Islamic Development Bank. Tunisia's socioeconomic development since 1990 and the challenges facing the country were assessed jointly; each institution's assistance program was evaluated in parallel.

Tunisia has successfully shifted from resource-based exports dominated by oil and gas to manufactures and services. The economy is now driven mainly by textile, electrical, mechanical, and food processing exports; tourism and related activities; and production of olives and cereals. Real GDP growth has been rising consistently, increasing from 3 percent annually over 1985–90 to more than 5 percent annually over 1996–02. Today, with a per capita income of US$2,000, Tunisians enjoy more than two-and-a-half times the real incomes that their parents had 30 years ago. Tunisia signed an association agreement with the European Union (EUAA) that provides for free trade in manufacturing by 2008. The European Union (EU) has been Tunisia's dominant trading partner; the region is the source of 67 percent of capital flows into Tunisia, accounts for a large share of Tunisia's tourism market, and is the region with the largest community of expatriate Tunisians. This dominance renders Tunisia's economy vulnerable to adverse developments in the EU.

Rapid growth made possible a remarkable improvement in social indicators and a decline in the poverty

RESUMEN

Esta Evaluación de Asistencia al País ha sido preparada en colaboración con el Banco Islámico de Desarrollo. Se llevó a cabo una evaluación conjunta del desarrollo socioeconómico de Túnez desde 1990 y de los desafíos que enfrenta el país; se evaluaron en paralelo los programas de asistencia de cada institución.

Túnez ha realizado con éxito el paso de exportaciones basadas en recursos (principalmente petróleo y gas) a las de manufacturas y servicios. En la actualidad, la economía está impulsada principalmente por las exportaciones textiles, electromecánicas y las relacionadas con el procesamiento de alimentos, así como por las actividades turísticas y afines y la producción de aceitunas y cereales. El PIB real ha crecido en forma constante, de un 3 por ciento anual entre 1985 y 1990 a más de un 5 por ciento anual entre 1996 y 2002. Hoy, con ingresos per cápita de USD 2.000, los ingresos reales de los tunecinos corresponden a dos veces y media los que obtenían sus padres hace treinta años. Túnez ha celebrado un acuerdo de asociación con la Unión Europea (EUAA, por sus siglas en inglés) que prevé la implementación del libre comercio de manufacturas para 2008. La Unión Europea (UE) ha sido el principal socio comercial de Túnez; la región es la fuente del 67 por ciento del flujo de capital hacia Túnez, representa una gran proporción del mercado del turismo en ese país y constituye la región con la mayor comunidad de

RÉSUMÉ

Cette Évaluation de l'aide au pays a été préparée en collaboration avec la Banque Islamique de Développement. Le développement social et économique de la Tunisie depuis 1990 et les défis auxquels le pays doit faire face ont été évalués conjointement ; chaque programme d'assistance des institutions a été évalué en parallèle.

La Tunisie est passée avec succès d'un pays dépendant essentiellement de ses exportations de pétrole et de gaz, à celui tirant ses ressources de produits manufacturés et de services. Son économie s'appuie dorénavant sur les exportations de textiles, d'équipements électriques et mécaniques, de l'industrie alimentaire, du tourisme et activités liées, et de la production d'olives et de céréales. La croissance du PIB réel est en progression constante : en hausse de 3 pour cent entre 1985 et 1990 à plus de 5 pour cent sur la période 1996-2002. Avec un revenu par habitant de 2000 USD, les Tunisiens jouissent aujourd'hui d'un revenu 2 fois et demi supérieur à celui de leurs parents trente ans plus tôt. Le pays a signé un accord d'association avec l'Union européenne (l'EUAA), instaurant des termes de libre-échange dans le secteur de la fabrication d'ici 2008. L'UE est le partenaire principal de la Tunisie ; la zone représente 67 pour cent des flux de capitaux en Tunisie ; elle joue un rôle important dans le marché du tourisme du pays et compte la plus importante communauté d'expatriés tunisiens. Par voie de conséquence,

ENGLISH

rate from 40 percent in 1970 to 4 percent in 2000; the remaining poverty is predominately rural. But if the vulnerable population just above the poverty line is included, the percentage of the poor would increase by another 6 percentage points to over 10 percent. Addressing vulnerability and rural poverty remains a priority, as does reconciling Bank and government estimates of the breakdown of poverty between rural and urban areas. Tunisia's social indicators are better, on average, than those of the Middle East and North Africa (MNA) Region and better than those of other lower-middle-income countries. Tunisia leads the MNA Region in gender equity. Challenges relate to sustaining higher growth, achieving closer integration with the EU, and improving efficiency of social services in the face of Tunisia's vulnerability to external shocks, its level of indebtedness, and the more competitive environment it will likely confront in the future.

The Bank's strategy since 1990, rooted in wide-ranging and influential analytic and advisory activities, was to support macroeconomic stabilization, pro-market structural reforms to foster growth, and social programs, as well as human development. The strategy was relevant to the government's priorities, outlined in a series of national development plans. An increased focus on the social sectors was aligned with the Millennium Development Goals (MDGs) and the country's emphasis on human resource development. The Bank lending program is large, both in per capita terms and as a share of the MNA portfolio. Annual average lending commitments for

ESPAÑOL

tunecinos expatriados. Por tal motivo, la economía es vulnerable a cualquier circunstancia adversa que pueda afectar a la UE.

El rápido crecimiento hizo posible una mejora notable en los indicadores sociales, así como una reducción en la tasa de pobreza, del 40 por ciento en 1970 al 4 por ciento en el año 2000; la pobreza que aún persiste es predominantemente rural. No obstante, si se incluyera a la población que se encuentra justo por encima de la línea de pobreza, el porcentaje de pobres se incrementaría en otros 6 puntos porcentuales, a más del 10 por ciento. La vulnerabilidad y la pobreza rural continúan siendo temas prioritarios, al igual que la conciliación de las estimaciones del Banco y el gobierno con respecto a la distribución de la pobreza en las áreas rurales y urbanas. En promedio, los indicadores sociales de Túnez superan al resto de la región del Medio Oriente y Norte de África (MENA) u otros países de ingreso mediano bajo; el país también es líder en esta región en cuanto a la igualdad de los géneros. Los desafíos que enfrenta consisten en poder sostener un crecimiento elevado, lograr una mayor integración con la UE y mejorar la eficiencia de los servicios sociales, en vista de la vulnerabilidad de Túnez ante golpes externos, su nivel de endeudamiento y el entorno más competitivo que probablemente deba enfrentar en el futuro.

Desde 1990, la estrategia del Banco, con base en actividades de análisis y asesoramiento influyentes y de gran alcance, consistió en apoyar la estabilización macroeconómica, así como las reformas estructurales para promover programas sociales y de crecimiento, y el desarrollo humano.

FRANÇAIS

l'économie tunisienne est sensible aux turbulences que peut connaître l'UE.

La croissance rapide de l'économie dans sa globalité a rendu possible une remarquable amélioration des indicateurs sociaux et un déclin du taux de pauvreté de 40 pour cent en 1970 à 4 pour cent en 2000 ; le bastion de la misère reste essentiellement rural. Néanmoins, si l'on inclut la population dans le besoin située juste au-dessus du seuil de pauvreté, le pourcentage des personnes démunies augmente de six points à plus de 10 pour cent. La lutte contre la précarité et la pauvreté rurale reste une priorité, tout comme la mise en concordance des évaluations de la Banque et du Gouvernement concernant les écarts de pauvreté observés entre les mondes rural et urbain. Les indicateurs sociaux de la Tunisie sont en moyenne plus favorables que ceux de la zone MOAN ou des autres pays à revenus moyens plus bas ; le pays se situe également en première position de la zone MOAN en ce qui concerne l'égalité des sexes. Les défis posés relèvent d'une croissance supérieure durable, d'une meilleure intégration au sein de l'UE et d'une plus grande efficacité des services sociaux face à la vulnérabilité de la Tunisie vis-à-vis des chocs externes, de son niveau d'endettement et d'une compétitivité accrue à laquelle elle devra probablement faire face à l'avenir.

La stratégie de la Banque depuis 1990, qui s'appuie sur un large éventail d'activités de conseil et d'analyses d'influence, a consisté à soutenir la stabilisation économique et les réformes structurelles en direction des marchés, de façon à encourager la croissance et les programmes sociaux

ENGLISH

fiscal years 1990–03 were US$200 million (or US$20 per capita per year), representing over one-quarter of the MNA Regional portfolio. Annual average net disbursements were only US$27 million, and net transfers were negative for most of the period. Policy-based lending, in conjunction with various donor programs, accounted for 40 percent of total lending and addressed trade, financial, and private sector development. Investment loans supported mainly rural and human development projects. The Bank served as a significant catalyst for mobilizing resources, leveraging nearly US$1 for every IBRD dollar.

With timely and effective support from the Bank and other donors, Tunisia averted a balance of payments crisis in the late 1980s, and since then has maintained a solid record of macroeconomic stability and remarkable socioeconomic progress. The main attributes of Tunisia's success were ownership and broad political consensus, a well-developed human resource base, and a stable macroeconomic environment. The Bank's programs successfully promoted policy reforms. Substantial financial sector reforms were achieved, as well as the removal of disincentives for investment and the privatization of public enterprises. Tariffs have been reduced and the economy is now more open to the outside world. Manufactured exports have grown steadily, increasing their share to 80 percent of exports. The overall soundness of the banking system has improved, as indicated by progress in prudential ratios. Privatization in the banking sector has also advanced.

ESPAÑOL

Esta estrategia era relevante para las prioridades del gobierno, planteadas en una serie de planes nacionales de desarrollo. La mayor atención a los sectores sociales era compatible con los Objetivos de Desarrollo del Milenio (ODM) y el énfasis del país en el desarrollo de los recursos humanos. El programa de financiamiento del Banco es importante, tanto en valores per cápita como en términos de la proporción que representa en la cartera para la región de Medio Oriente y Norte de África. Los compromisos de financiamiento anual promedio para los ejercicios fiscales de 1990 a 2003 fueron de USD 200 millones (o USD 20 per cápita por año); esto representa más de un cuarto de la cartera regional. Los desembolsos netos anuales promedio fueron de sólo USD 27 millones, y las transferencias netas fueron negativas para la mayor parte del período. El financiamiento basado en políticas, conjuntamente con diversos programas de donantes, representó un 40 por ciento del financiamiento total y se destinó al desarrollo comercial, financiero y del sector privado. Los préstamos para inversión se destinaron a apoyar principalmente proyectos de desarrollo rural y humano. El Banco tuvo una importante función catalizadora al movilizar recursos a razón de USD 1 por cada dólar del BIRF.

A fines de la década de 1980, con un apoyo oportuno y eficaz del Banco y otros donantes, Túnez evitó una crisis de la balanza de pagos, y desde entonces ha mantenido un historial sólido de estabilidad macroeconómica y un notable progreso socioeconómico. Los factores principales del éxito de Túnez han sido la identificación con los programas y el amplio consenso polí-

FRANÇAIS

ainsi que le développement humain. Elle s'est révélée pertinente en ce qui concerne les priorités du Gouvernement qui ont été soulignées dans une série de plans de développement nationaux. L'attention particulière portée aux secteurs sociaux s'est alignée sur les objectifs de développement pour le millénaire (MDG) et sur l'engagement du pays en faveur du développement des ressources humaines. Le programme de prêt de la Banque représente une contribution substantielle, à la fois par habitant et comme part du portefeuille de la zone MOAN. Les efforts annuels moyens consentis pour les années fiscales de la période 1990–2003 ont atteint les 200 millions USD (20 USD par habitant et par an), soit plus du quart du portefeuille régional. Les versements moyens nets annuels se sont élevés à 27 millions USD ; cependant, les transferts nets ont été négatifs pendant la plus grande partie de la période. Les prêts fondés sur les politiques, associés aux différents programmes des bailleurs, ont représenté 40 pour cent du total des prêts et du développement des échanges commerciaux, du secteur financier et privé. Ceux liés à l'investissement ont soutenu les projets de développement principalement ruraux et humains. La Banque a servi de puissant catalyseur dans la mobilisation des ressources, en permettant de lever presque 1 USD pour chaque dollar de la BIRD.

Grâce au soutien effectif et en temps utile de la Banque et d'autres donateurs, la Tunisie a pu éviter une crise de sa balance des paiements à la fin des années 80. Dès lors, elle a enregistré des chiffres solides en matière de stabilité macroéconomique et des progrès socioéconomiques re-

ENGLISH

Bank assistance also contributed to significant progress in the rural and social sectors. The Bank's major contribution in the rural sector was in putting Tunisian agriculture on the path of liberalization, supporting reform measures that contributed to increasing farm incomes in remote areas, and improving resource management sustainability. With Bank support, Tunisia made impressive progress in almost all areas covered by the MDGs, already meeting some targets—and the country is likely to meet others by 2015. For example, by the mid-1990s, almost all children attended school, meeting the MDG of universal primary education. Overall, the outcome of the Bank's assistance program is rated satisfactory, based on its substantial relevance and efficacy. Institutional capacity was strengthened further with the Bank's support, and institutional development impact is rated substantial.

Despite significant development progress and the satisfactory outcome of the Bank's assistance program, shortfalls in some areas, combined with the more competitive environment that Tunisia will likely face in the future, pose risks to sustaining its remarkable development performance. Both the low rate of private investment and the inefficiency of overall investment are indicators that past growth may be difficult to sustain without deeper reform. One area where progress remained below Bank expectations was that of promoting private sector development; the government still plays a significant role in economic activity. In the financial sector, public banks remain large in terms of as-

ESPAÑOL

tico, así como una base de recursos humanos calificada y un entorno macroeconómico estable. Los programas del Banco promovieron con éxito las reformas a las políticas. Se lograron reformas sustanciales en el sector financiero, así como la eliminación de desincentivos para la inversión y la privatización de empresas públicas. Se redujeron las tarifas, y la economía está ahora más abierta al mundo. Las exportaciones de manufacturas han experimentado un crecimiento sostenido, hasta representar un 80 por ciento del total. La solidez general del sistema bancario ha mejorado, como lo indica el avance de los coeficientes prudenciales. La privatización del sector bancario también ha experimentado avances. La asistencia del Banco contribuyó asimismo a un progreso significativo en los sectores social y rural. El principal aporte del Banco al sector rural fue poner a la agricultura de Túnez en el camino de la liberalización, apoyando reformas que contribuyeron a incrementar los ingresos agrícolas en áreas remotas y a mejorar la sostenibilidad de la gestión de recursos. Con el apoyo del Banco, Túnez hizo avances notables en casi todas las áreas de los ODM, pues ya ha alcanzado algunos objetivos, y probablemente cumpla otros para el año 2015. Por ejemplo, para mediados de la década de 1990 casi todos los niños habían asistido a la escuela, con lo que se cumplió la ODM de la educación primaria universal. En términos generales, el resultado del programa de asistencia del Banco se considera satisfactorio, debido a su relevancia y su eficacia sustanciales. La capacidad institucional se fortaleció aún más con el apoyo del Banco, y se considera que ha habido un impacto sustancial sobre el desarrollo institucional.

FRANÇAIS

marquables. Les principaux points forts de sa réussite résident dans une forte implication et un large consensus politique, des ressources humaines bien développées et un environnement macroéconomique stable. Les programmes de la Banque ont appuyé avec succès les réformes de politique. Les évolutions importantes du secteur financier ont été menées à bien, de même que la mise à l'écart des facteurs défavorables aux investissements et à la privatisation des entreprises publiques. Les droits de douane ont été réduits et l'économie est dorénavant plus ouverte au monde extérieur. Les exportations de produits manufacturées ont augmenté de façon régulière et leur part représente aujourd'hui 80 pour cent. La crédibilité générale du système bancaire s'est améliorée, comme l'indique l'évolution favorable des ratios prudentiels. La privatisation du secteur bancaire a également avancé. Par ailleurs, l'assistance de la Banque a entraîné des améliorations notables dans les secteurs ruraux et sociaux. Sa contribution majeure dans le secteur rural a consisté à engager l'agriculture tunisienne sur la voie de la libéralisation, en soutenant les réformes qui ont contribué à augmenter les revenus des exploitations agricoles dans les régions les plus reculées et à améliorer la durabilité de la gestion des ressources. Grâce au soutien de la Banque, des progrès remarquables ont été réalisés dans la quasi-totalité des domaines couverts par les MDG, en atteignant d'ores et déjà certains objectifs. Les autres le seront probablement d'ici 2015. On constate ainsi que, dès le milieu des années 90, la plupart des enfants sont scolarisés, ce qui répond à l'objectif

ENGLISH

sets, and nonperforming loans impose a heavy burden on the sector and pose risks to stability. In trade policy, tariff rates remain above competitors' levels, and more needs to be done to ensure that discrimination against non-EU trade is eliminated within the overall framework of the EUAA.

Another area where the government's program needs to be enhanced and the Bank needs to direct greater attention is the overall efficiency and fiscal sustainability of social expenditures, as expenditures on social services remain high. Education expansion at the post-basic level and a decline in basic education enrollment because of demographic changes will necessitate efficiency improvements. In the rural sector, addressing issues such as land tenure, rural finance, non-farm rural development, and research and extension will be important, as these are areas where past Bank assistance programs were less successful. Finally, past positive development outcomes have fostered a large middle class that will press for more participation in the development process. In the past, Tunisia has managed well its economic and regional political uncertainties by maintaining social and macroeconomic stability, gradually diversifying its export base, and forging closer relations with the EU. Given its past record, sustainability of these achievements is rated likely.

This evaluation recommends that the Bank continue to support improving the environment for private sector development and enhancing competitiveness, as the country seeks to integrate more into the global economy and will confront an increasingly competitive climate

ESPAÑOL

Pese a los avances significativos en el desarrollo y al resultado satisfactorio del programa de asistencia del Banco, las deficiencias en algunas áreas, combinadas con el entorno más competitivo que Túnez posiblemente enfrente en el futuro, plantean riesgos para la sostenibilidad de su destacado desarrollo. Tanto la baja tasa de inversión privada como la ineficiencia de las inversiones en general indican que el crecimiento pasado posiblemente sea difícil de mantener si no se profundiza la reforma. Un área en la que el progreso no satisfizo las expectativas del Banco fue la promoción del desarrollo del sector privado; el gobierno continúa desempeñando un papel significativo en la actividad económica. En el sector financiero, los bancos públicos siguen estando sobredimensionados en términos de activos, y los préstamos no redituables representan una carga pesada para el sector, además de constituir un riesgo para la estabilidad. En materia de política comercial, los aranceles siguen estando por encima de los niveles de los competidores, y es necesario tomar más medidas tendientes a eliminar la discriminación contra el comercio proveniente de países fuera de la UE, dentro del marco general del EUAA. Otra área en la que es necesario mejorar el programa del gobierno, y a la que el Banco necesita prestar más atención que en el pasado, es la eficiencia general y la sostenibilidad fiscal del gasto social, pues el gasto en servicios sociales sigue siendo elevado. La expansión de la educación en el nivel posterior al básico, conjugada con la declinación en la inscripción en la educación básica debido a cambios demográficos,

FRANÇAIS

d'éducation primaire pour tous. Globalement, le résultat du programme d'assistance de la Banque est jugé satisfaisant. La capacité institutionnelle a pu être une nouvelle fois renforcée grâce à son soutien, et l'impact du développement institutionnel est estimé substantiel.

En dépit de progrès significatifs en matière de développement et des résultats encourageants du programme d'assistance, certains domaines laissent apparaître des failles qui, combinées à un environnement toujours plus compétitif auxquels la Tunisie sera probablement confrontée à l'avenir, menacent les remarquables performances de développement. Le taux d'investissement privé peu élevé et, plus généralement, le manque d'efficacité des investissements, indiquent qu'il sera sans doute difficile de maintenir la croissance sans envisager de profondes réformes. La promotion du développement du secteur privé est l'un des domaines où les progrès restent en deçà des attentes de la Banque car le Gouvernement joue encore un rôle non négligeable dans l'activité économique. Dans le secteur financier, les banques publiques sont importantes en termes d'actifs. Les prêts non-productifs (NPL) imposent une charge lourde sur le secteur et engendrent des risques pour la stabilité. En ce qui concerne la politique des échanges commerciaux, les taux des droits de douane restent supérieurs à ceux des concurrents. De nouvelles mesures doivent être engagées afin de garantir la levée de toute discrimination dans le cadre général de l'EUAA, vis-à-vis des échanges hors zone européenne. Un autre domaine où le programme de l'État a besoin d'être développé et sur lequel la Banque doit diriger davantage son at-

ENGLISH

in the next few years. Adopting a results-based approach, with agreed and monitorable output and outcome indicators embedded in an improved monitoring and evaluation framework, would help to anchor the Bank's assistance program in the future. Specifically, the Bank should (i) help the country pursue trade openness with the EU and the rest of the world; (ii) help improve the business environment through regulatory and judiciary reforms, including measures to reduce the flow and stock of nonperforming loans; and (iii) promote enterprise and financial sector privatization. Future Bank programs should also (iv) help strengthen rural institutions to support efficient output and input markets (for example, land and rural finance) while maintaining social and political stability through better-targeted safety nets. After 21 years without a rural sectorwide review, the Bank should undertake one to inform its future programs. Finally, the Bank should also fill the gaps in core diagnostic economic and sector work (ESW) by completing a Public Expenditure Review (PER), a Country Financial Accountability Assessment (CFAA), and a Country Procurement Assessment Review (CPAR). In particular, a PER could help build capacity to prioritize public spending and provide the basis for measures to efficiently address education expansion.

ESPAÑOL

harán necesaria la implementación de mejoras orientadas a la eficiencia. En el sector rural será importante abordar temas como la tenencia de tierras, el financiamiento del sector rural, el desarrollo rural no agrícola y la investigación y extensión, pues son áreas en las que los programas de asistencia anteriores del Banco han tenido menos éxito. Por último, los resultados positivos del pasado en el área del desarrollo han promovido la formación de una gran clase media que ejercerá presión para lograr una mayor participación en el proceso de desarrollo. En el pasado, Túnez ha tenido se ha manejado bien ante la incertidumbre económica y política regional, manteniendo la estabilidad social y macroeconómica, diversificando gradualmente su base de exportaciones y forjando relaciones más estrechas con la UE. A la luz de sus antecedentes, se considera probable que pueda sostener sus logros.

Esta evaluación recomienda que el Banco continúe apoyando las mejoras coyunturales para el desarrollo del sector privado y el aumento de la competitividad, dado que el país procura profundizar su integración a la economía global, y probablemente deba enfrentar un clima cada vez más competitivo en los años venideros. La adopción de un enfoque orientado a los resultados, con indicadores de productos y resultados acordados en un entorno mejorado de seguimiento y evaluación, ayudaría a forjar una base firme para el programa de asistencia del Banco en el futuro. Específicamente, el Banco debería (i) ayudar al país a procurar lograr la apertura comercial con la UE y el resto del mundo, (ii) contribuir a mejorar el entorno comercial mediante

FRANÇAIS

tention est celui de l'efficacité globale et de la durabilité de la politique budgétaire des dépenses sociales, celles concernant les services sociaux restant élevées. Le développement de l'éducation à un niveau post-basique et le recul du recrutement dans l'éducation de base dû à des évolutions démographiques nécessiteront une meilleure efficacité. Dans le secteur rural, la résolution de problèmes tels que l'accession à la propriété foncière, le financement rural, le développement du monde rural non-agricole, la recherche et la vulgarisation, sera essentielle, puisque ces domaines s'avèrent être ceux dans lesquels les programmes d'assistance antérieurs de la Banque ont connu le moins de succès. Enfin, les résultats antérieurs positifs en termes de développement ont nourri une importante classe moyenne qui insistera sur sa participation accrue dans le processus de développement par le biais d'un rôle plus important de la société civile et du secteur privé. Par le passé, la Tunisie a su gérer les incertitudes politiques régionales et économiques en maintenant une stabilité macroéconomique et sociale, en diversifiant progressivement ses exportations de base et en instaurant des relations plus privilégiées avec l'UE. De ce fait, la durabilité de ces progrès est jugée probable.

La présente évaluation recommande que la Banque poursuive son soutien en direction d'une amélioration des conditions nécessaires au développement du secteur privé et d'une augmentation de la compétitivité, le pays visant une plus grande intégration au sein de l'économie mondiale et s'exposant à un environnement toujours plus compétitif dans les années à venir. Une approche s'appuyant sur des conclusions recon-

ESPAÑOL

reformas regulatorias y jurídicas, por ejemplo con medidas para reducir el flujo y la cantidad de préstamos no redituables, y (iii) promover la privatización del sector financiero y de las empresas públicas. Los programas futuros del Banco deberían, además, (iv) ayudar a fortalecer las instituciones rurales a fin de dar apoyo a los mercados eficientes de productos e insumos (por ejemplo, el financiamiento rural y de adquisición de tierras) manteniendo a la vez la estabilidad social y política a través de redes de seguridad mejor orientadas. Después de 21 años sin realizar un examen con alcance a todo el sector rural, el Banco debería llevarlo a cabo para informar sus futuros programas. Por último, el Banco también debería llenar el vacío existente en materia de trabajos básicos de diagnóstico con estudios económicos y sectoriales, mediante una Revisión del Gasto Público, una Evaluación de la Capacidad de Gestión Financiera y una Evaluación de las Contrataciones del País. En particular, el estudio del gasto público podría ayudar a fortalecer las capacidades para priorizar el gasto público y proporcionar un parámetro de medición para abordar con eficiencia la expansión de la educación.

FRANÇAIS

nues et vérifiables et sur des indicateurs de réalisation et de résultats ayant bénéficié eux-mêmes d'un meilleur encadrement en termes de suivi et d'évaluation, contribuera à ancrer le programme d'aide de la Banque à l'avenir. Plus précisément, la Banque doit (i) assister le pays afin qu'il poursuive son ouverture aux échanges commerciaux avec l'UE et le reste du monde, (ii) l'aider à améliorer l'environnement des affaires par le biais de réformes ayant trait aux réglementations et au cadre juridique, en incluant des mesures visant à réduire les flux et les stocks des NPL, et (iii) promouvoir la privatisation du secteur entrepreuneurial et financier. Les programmes futurs de la Banque doivent également contribuer au renforcement des institutions rurales de manière à soutenir les marchés d'intrants et d'extrants rentables (par exemple, le financement de la propriété foncière et du monde rural), tout en maintenant une stabilité sociale et politique via de meilleurs réseaux de sécurité ciblés. La Banque doit pallier à 21 années d'absence d'étude large du secteur rural pour mieux asseoir ses programmes à venir. Enfin, elle doit également combler les lacunes du diagnostic de fond du TES : Revues des dépenses publiques (PER), Évaluation des système de gestion des finances publiques (CFAA) et Évaluation du système de passation des marchés publics (CPAR). En particulier, une PER pourrait contribuer à donner priorité aux dépenses publiques et apporter les bases d'outils de mesures permettant de s'atteler efficacement au développement de l'éducation.

Gregory K. Ingram
Director-General, Operations Evaluation

ACRONYMS AND ABBREVIATIONS

AAA	Analytical and advisory activities
AAL	Agricultural Adjustment Loan
AFD	Agence Française de Développement (French Development Agency)
AfDB	African Development Bank
ASIL	Agricultural Sector Investment Loan
BNA	Banque Nationale Agricole
BNP	Banque Nationale de Paris
CAE	Country Assistance Evaluation
CAS	Country Assistance Strategy
CEM	Country Economic Memorandum
CFAA	Country Financial Accountability Assessment
CPAR	Country Procurement Assessment Review
ECAL	Economic Competitiveness Adjustment Loan
EFRSL	Enterprise and Financial Reform Support Loan
EIB	European Investment Bank
ESW	Economic and sector work
EQIP	Education Quality Improvement Program
EU	European Union
EUAA	European Union Association Agreement
FDI	Foreign Direct Investment
FSD	Financial sector development
GDP	Gross domestic product
GNI	Gross national income
GNP	Gross national product
GOT	Government of Tunisia
GSM	Global System Mobile
IBRD	International Bank for Reconstruction and Development
IDB	Islamic Development Bank
IMF	International Monetary Fund
INS	Institut Nationale des Statistiques (National Institute of Statistics)
ITPAL	Industry and Trade Policy Adjustment Loan
KfW	Kreditanstalt für Wiederaufbau (German Agency for Reconstruction)
M&E	Monitoring and evaluation
MDG	Millennium Development Goal
MEDA	Mesures d'accompagnement financiers et techniques à la reforme des structures économiques et sociales dans le cadre du partenariat euro-méditerranéen
MFA	Multifibre Arrangement
MM	Macroeconomic management
MNA	Middle East and North Africa Region
MOA	Ministry of Agriculture
MOE	Ministry of Education
NGO	Nongovernmental organization
NPL	Nonperforming loans
ODESYPANO	Office du Développement Sylvo-Pastoral du Nord-Ouest
OECD	Organisation for Economic Co-operation and Development
OED	Operations Evaluation Department

PE	Public enterprise
PER	Public Expenditure Review
PERL	Public Enterprise Restructuring Loan
PPAR	Project Performance Assessment Report
QAG	Quality Assurance Group
QR	Quantitative restrictions
SAL	Structural Adjustment Loan
SDR	Special Drawing Rights
SMEs	Small and medium-size enterprises
UNDP	United Nations Development Program
VAT	Value added tax
WSIP	Water Sector Investment Project
WTO	World Trade Organization

Tunisia's Socioeconomic Development

Progress Achieved and Challenges Ahead

This Country Assistance Evaluation (CAE) looks at the effectiveness of World Bank assistance since 1990 from three perspectives: an analysis of the Bank's assistance program, the Bank's development impact, and the contribution of the Bank and its development partners to development outcomes. Annex C describes the methodology. The evaluation is based on background studies, internal World Bank reports, and interviews with government officials, Bank staff, donors, and civil society. Annex B contains a list of the people interviewed. The CAE was prepared in collaboration with the Islamic Development Bank.

Background

Tunisia gained its independence from France in 1956. As a republic with a strong central authority vested in the president, it has since experienced political stability at a time when its neighborhood has been experiencing significant turmoil. As a moderate Arab country in North Africa, it has managed not to be absorbed within the vortex of the more complex Middle Eastern politics, while maintaining a good link with its Arab neighbors, often serving as an interlocutor or a political haven. The United States announced the opening in 2004 of a regional office in Tunis of the U.S.–Middle East Partnership Initiative. As with its neighbors in North Africa, much of

Tunisia's land is arid, or semi-arid, with as little as 3 percent of arable land irrigated, while rain-fed agriculture is subject to severe annual fluctuations in rainfall. In 2002, the population of 9.8 million had a per capita income of US$2,000 (annex table A.1).

After independence, the political leadership opted initially for a *dirigiste* economic system, with mainly public ownership of manufacturing industries, banks, and other financial institutions. At independence, the country's most important raw materials were petroleum, natural gas, and phosphates. However, oil and gas production has been decreasing as reserves have been depleted, and the quality of phosphate deposits is poor. As an alternative

1

source of income, attention has been given to the development of manufacturing, tourism, and other services. At the same time, the country invested heavily in human resource development and paid particular attention to welfare and education. This proved an important contributor to Tunisia's economic performance in subsequent decades.

The oil boom of the 1970s. The multifold increase in the price of crude generated high export revenues that financed significantly higher levels of investment (30 percent of GDP), particularly in manufacturing. As a result, real GDP growth averaged 7.4 percent annually throughout the 1970s. High oil revenues allowed the economy to perform well under the dirigiste system. Directive policies controlling investment and prices were broadly applied, in the context of protected trade and generous subsidies to enterprises. The priority given to human resource development continued.

The first half of the 1980s: decline and apprehension. Problems with economic performance started to emerge in the early 1980s as oil prices and production levels declined, while high investment levels and public expenditures were maintained. Although Tunisia's Sixth Five-Year Plan (1982–86) proposed stringent policies, unaffordable investment levels and lax policies continued, leading to a deterioration in the macroeconomic situation. By 1984, inflation had risen to 10 percent; the current account deficit had grown to almost 11 percent of GDP, external debt to 46 percent of GDP, and the debt service ratio to 21 percent. By 1985, a balance of payment crisis appeared imminent.

The turning point in the mid-1980s. Faced with growing macroeconomic imbalances, the government pursued a program of stabilization and adjustment supported by the World Bank and the International Monetary Fund (IMF). The reform program proceeded at a gradual but steady pace, consolidating past

Today, Tunisians enjoy more than two-and-a-half times the real incomes that their parents had 30 years ago.

progress, although the state continued to keep a prominent position in the economy. The fiscal deficit and inflation fell, and GDP grew at 4 percent per annum between 1987 and 1994. The fiscal and current account deficits have hovered around 4 percent of GDP since the mid-1990s.

A new phase of development by the mid-1990s. Given Tunisia's limited domestic markets, the government decided to increase its integration in the world economy to accelerate higher growth. In 1995, Tunisia became the first country in the region to sign an association agreement with the European Union (EUAA). The agreement includes provisions for the phased establishment of a free trade zone for manufacturers over a 12-year period (1996–08). Also, Tunisia signed bilateral trade agreements with Morocco, Jordan, Libya, Iraq, and Syria. The economy is now more open to the outside world, and imports and exports constitute about 90 percent of GDP, up from 70 percent in the mid-1980s. This ratio compares favorably to other Middle East and North Africa (MNA) Region countries at similar income levels (annex table A.2k).

From oil-dominated and volatile to more stable and diversified economy. Since the mid-1980s, Tunisia's exports have been successfully diversified, moving away from resource-based exports dominated by oil and gas to manufactures (table 1.1). Export of manufactures has grown at around 10 percent a year in real terms since 1987, increasing the share of manufactures in exports to over 80 percent. Tunisia's economy is now driven mainly by textiles, electrical and mechanical equipment, and food processing (in the manufacturing sector); tourism and related activities (in the services sector); and production of olives and cereals (in the agricultural sector). Tunisia's major exports are now textiles and leather (making up 50 percent of exports). Today, Tunisians enjoy more than two-and-a-half times the real incomes that their parents had 30 years ago. The service sector, which accounts for nearly 60 percent of GDP, has been providing the largest contribution. The industrial sector is the second largest, with about 28 percent of GDP, and has been fairly dynamic. Agriculture's contri-

Table 1.1	Tunisia's Export Diversification, 1980–01		
	1980	**1987**	**2001**
Oil products	**52.5**	**23.5**	**9.2**
Non-oil products	**47.5**	**76.4**	**90.8**
Manufactures	35.7	60.3	80.7
Chemicals	13.2	18.1	10.0
Machinery and transport equipment	2.4	6.1	15.4
Food	7.2	12.7	7.9

Source: U.N. Comtrade Database; data refer to percentage ratio.

bution to growth fluctuates widely, largely based on weather conditions. Nevertheless, agriculture remains a major sector in the economy, employing about one-fourth of the labor force and accounting for almost 12 percent of GDP in 2001.

Economic and social performance since the late 1980s. Tunisia has achieved very good economic and social performance by maintaining a stable macroeconomic framework, placing strong emphasis on social achievement, and implementing—although gradually—structural reforms. Table 1.2 reflects progress in macroeconomic performance; tables 1.3 and 1.4 show progress in poverty reduction and social development.

Poverty and Social Conditions

Poverty reduction. Tunisia has made remarkable progress in reducing poverty. The Bank's estimate of Tunisia's incidence of poverty, as measured by the head count index, dropped from 40 percent of the population in 1970 to 11 percent by 1985, to 8 percent by 1990, and to 4 percent by 2000 (table 1.3). Although rural poverty has also decreased over the years, its level has remained twice the national average. However, there is controversy about the rural poverty incidence (chapter 3). The rural population comprises 35 to 40 percent of the population, and the rural poor derive their incomes primarily from agricultural activities, which are subject to large fluctuations. These fluctuations have a strong impact on the economy. A one percentage point decrease in agriculture causes a 0.25 percent decline in overall GDP, stemming from significant indirect effects on manufacturing and service activities that have a linkage with agriculture. The share

Tunisia has made remarkable progress in reducing poverty.

Table 1.2	Main Macroeconomic Indicators					
Indicator	1986–90	1991–95	1996–00	2001	2002	Est. 2003
GDP growth (%, real GDP at market price)	2.9	3.9	5.6	4.9	1.7	5.5
Inflation (%, CPI Index)	7.1	5.8	3.4	2.7	2.3	2.1
Real effective exchange rate (REER) index (1990=100)	107.9	102.6	104.2	100.9	99.7	—
Budget deficit (% GDP)	3.8	3.7	3.7	3.8	3.5	3.1
Current account deficit (% GDP)	3.9	5.8	3.1	4.7	3.5	3.1
Foreign direct investment (% GDP)	0.8	1.6	2.6	2.2	3.8	2.1
Total public debt (% GDP)	62.0	60.7	59.4	60.2	64.3	60.2
Gross foreign reserves (months of imports c.i.f.)	1.9	1.8	2.9	2.5	2.9	2.9

Source: Calculations based on data from the World Bank (2000b) and IMF data.

Table 1.3	Poverty and Inequality Trends in Tunisia, 1990–2000								
	1990			**1995**			**2000**		
	National	**Rural**	**Urban**	**National**	**Rural**	**Urban**	**National**	**Rural**	**Urban**
Incidence: National Headcount Index (% of population)	7.9	14.8	3.3	8.1	15.8	3.2	4.1	8.3	1.7
Inequality: Gini coefficient	0.40	0.35	0.37	0.42	0.35	0.39	0.41	0.36	0.39

Source: Bank staff estimate for 2000 and World Bank 2000c, box 1, page 6.

Table 1.4	Selected Human Development Indicators in Tunisia and Comparator Countries				
Indicator	**Tunisia**		**MNA**		**Lower-middle-income countries**
	1970–75	**2000–01**	**1970–75**	**2000–01**	**2000–01**
Life expectancy (years)	55	72	46	68	69
Total fertility rate (births per woman)	5	2	6.6	3	2
Infant mortality (per thousand births)	94	26	125	43	33
Gross primary enrollment (% of school-age population)	72	119	69	97	107
Male	79	123	..	103	107
Female	65	116	..	90	107
Gross secondary enrollment (% of age group)	22	73	29	64	70
Adult illiteracy (% of population 15 years and above)	64	28	67	34	15
Male	51	18	56	24	9
Female	77	39	77	46	21

Note: Data refer to the most recent year available during the period specified.

Source: World Bank, *World Development Indicators* (various issues); details in Annex A, tables A.2d and A.2e.

of the poor and vulnerable people in the total population—as measured by the number of people having expenditures both below and about 30 percent above the poverty line—rose from 14 percent in 1990 to 17 percent in 1995, before falling to 10 percent in 2000. Addressing this vulnerability and targeting anti-poverty interventions becomes more difficult as poverty incidence falls.

Social achievement. Tunisia has made impressive achievements in human development in the past 30 years. Life expectancy has grown from 55 to 72 years; adult illiteracy has decreased from 64 to 28 percent; and infant mortality has dropped by nearly two-thirds (table 1.4). By the

mid-1990s, Tunisia had succeeded in enrolling almost all of the country's six-year-olds in first grade, meeting the Millennium Development Goal (MDG) of universal primary education. Tunisia's social indicators are better than the average of MNA countries, as well as of other lower-middle-income countries. The UNDP *Human Development Report* for 2003 ranks Tunisia ninety-first out of 175 countries on the human development index, ahead of other MNA countries at similar income levels (UNDP 2003).

Gender equity. Tunisia leads the MNA Region with regard to gender equity (table 1.4). The gap between girls and boys in basic education is low, and more than half of all university students are women. Compulsory education for girls and boys through ninth grade has helped bridge the gap between female and male school enrollment rates. The status of women has improved steadily, with rates of female labor force participation that are higher than those of other countries in the Region, but at 32 percent (in 2001), low compared with other lower-middle-income countries (World Bank data, 2003). Tunisia's female participation rate in the workforce increased by 4 percentage points during the 1990s. Tunisian women received the right to vote immediately after independence in 1957, before the women of many other MNA countries; the proportion of seats held by women in the national parliament was 12 percent in 2001. Tunisia ranks above the MNA average on the United Nations Gender Development Index (GDI).[1] As indicated earlier, this was due to the direct attention given to human resource development, with particular emphasis on gender equity.

Further progress in the social sectors is required to consolidate past gains and prepare Tunisia for a more competitive environment in the twenty-first century. There is still room for enhancing the quality and efficiency of social achievements. For example, the school system is still burdened with high dropout and repetition rates in the upper grades. Adult illiteracy rates remain high. Public health resources are not used efficiently (as evidenced by low rates of use of public health services), and the quality of services does not meet the population's expectations. Social progress has been achieved at a high cost relative to comparator countries: public expenditures on education are 7.7 percent of GNP compared with a MNA average of 5.2 percent and a lower-middle-income-country average of 4.9 percent (World Bank 2000b). Similarly, Tunisia's health expenditures of 5.5 percent of GDP are higher than the MNA average of 4.6 percent (World Bank data, 2003).

Debt Burden and External Assistance

Despite its remarkable economic progress and ability to weather past shocks, Tunisia's economy remains vulnerable to external shocks. The ratio of external debt to GDP is relatively high, hovering around 60 percent (table 1.2), and the U.S. dollar, with a share of over 40 percent, dominates the currency composition of this debt. These factors, together with the current account and budget deficits, make the country vulnerable to external shocks. Furthermore, foreign exchange reserves have remained low (below three months of imports). The economy weathered past shocks well (for example, the continued aftermath of September 11, 2001, events and a terrorist attack in Djerba, which led to a sharp drop in tourism) in terms of maintaining macro balances. However, the transition to greater integration into global markets raises challenges for debt sustainability because of competitive pressures and increased exposure to volatility.[2] Tunisia has recently been trying to diversify the currency composition of its debt by issuing euro-dominated sovereign bonds, as it did in July 1999. Also, the government is gradually shifting from external to domestic sources of financing.

Tunisia received large net financial flows (including grants and private flows) averaging nearly US$700 million annually (3.5 percent of GDP) over the 1990–01 period (table 1.5). In per capita terms, Tunisia received an annual average of US$70 per capita in net flows, below those for other MNA countries at similar income levels. The Bank has provided significant assistance to Tunisia, committing US$2.7 billion for 40 loans since 1990. With old loans being serviced and repaid, the Bank's share of net flows to Tunisia is about 5 percent. Since 1996, European Union (EU) member states have provided increased assistance to support the implementation of Tunisia's association agreement of 1995. The

Compulsory education for girls and boys through ninth grade has helped bridge the gap between female and male school enrollment rates.

Further progress in the social sectors is required to consolidate past gains and prepare Tunisia for a more competitive environment in the twenty-first century.

Table 1.5	Tunisia: Net Receipts of External Financial Resources, 1990–01 (yearly averages)					
	1990–01		**1990–95**		**1996–01**	
	$m	%	$m	%	$m	%
Total receipts, net[a]	689	100	762	100	615	100
IBRD	33	5	48	6	18	3
EC/ EU	347	50	280	37	413	67
France	98	14	64	8	132	21
Germany	26	4	26	4	23	4
Japan	100	15	100	13	100	16
United States	62	9	128	17	−4	−1
Arab countries and agencies	3	0	17	2	−10	−2

a. Total includes both official and private flows, from all sources, excluding the Islamic Development Bank.

Source: OECD (2003), as detailed in Annex A, table A.3a.

share of the EU and France nearly doubled in the 1996–01 period. Also, Tunisia is one of the largest recipients of Islamic Development Bank (IDB) assistance, with $1.2 billion in financing since 1976 (or about US$2 per capita per year).

Meeting the Challenges of Globalization

Increasing competitive pressures. The Tunisian economy will face increasing competitive pressures with the implementation of the EUAA and the elimination of the Multifiber Agreement (MFA). Tunisia's economy is open, but it is dependent on one dominant market (the EU) and on a few products (e.g., textiles account for 42 percent of exports). More than 75 percent of Tunisia's trade is currently with the EU, the region is the source of 67 percent of the capital that flows into Tunisia, it accounts for a large share of Tunisia's tourism market, and it has a large number of expatriate Tunisians (600,000). Therefore, economic conditions in the EU affect both external demand for Tunisia's products and domestic demand (through workers' remittances and tourism receipts). The economic opening—agreed with the EU over a 12-year period beginning in 1996—poses further challenges: dismantling tariffs, liberalizing the service sector, and establishing a free trade zone for manufactures by 2008. Tunisian producers will face much stronger competition in the local market with the implementation of

the EUAA and in their export markets after the elimination of the MFA. Since Tunisia's domestic market is small, investment and growth will depend critically on greater export competitiveness and further integration into the global market.

The role of the state in a rapidly changing world scene. The prudent and gradual approach—which has produced positive development outcomes—is now likely to have reached its limit under new developments in the international markets. The demise of the MFA and full implementation of the EUAA in the next few years impart some urgency to the need to accelerate reforms to enhance competitiveness and integration into the global economy. The government still involves itself in economic activities, with a public investment share of GDP at 13 percent, and still owns significant shares of the financial sector and public enterprises, which the government views as necessary to preserve social cohesion. One such program is the *mise à niveau* program (box 1.1). The World Bank has reservations about the program's efficacy and the distorted incentives it encourages. More important, the response of private investment to the policy measures has not been as strong as expected. Tunisia's private gross fixed investment remains low: averaging 13.5 percent of GDP during 1997–01, up moderately from 13 percent over 1990–96 (World Bank data,

2003) because of the slow pace of reform. Public investment accounts for another 13 percent of GDP. The high and persistent unemployment rate (14.3 percent in 2003) highlights the need to strengthen investment to sustain higher growth and generate jobs under increasing competitive pressures. As such, sustaining Tunisia's positive economic performance in the more competitive environment that it is likely to face in the next decade will likely require reducing the government's role in economic activity, as well as continuing to improve the design and operational efficiency of the regulatory and incentives regime, with the objective of leveling the playing field within the private sector. Past positive development outcomes have fostered a large middle class (80 percent of the population) that will press for greater participation in the development process through an increased role for civil society and the private sector.

The demise of the MFA and full implementation of the EUAA in the next few years impart some urgency to the need to accelerate reforms to enhance competitiveness and integration into the global economy.

Box 1.1	*Mise à niveau* Program (Enterprise Restructuring and Upgrading)

Mise à niveau program and the Government Ninth Development Plan (1997–01). The Ninth Development Plan aimed at improving business conditions and competitiveness. Within this framework, the *mise à niveau* program targeted the modernization of industrial infrastructure by adopting new technology, promoting quality, and training workers. The program finances: (i) upgrading and modernization of equipment, for which the subsidy covers 10 to 20 percent of the cost; (ii) the cost of "intangibles" (e.g., consultants and software), for which the subsidy covers up to 70 percent of the cost; and (c) financial restructuring, for which no subsidy is provided.

Mise à niveau program coverage. This program started in 1996 and has been targeted at small and medium-size enterprises (SMEs)—that is, enterprises with more than 10 employees. So far, 2,700 of approximately 3,600 eligible enterprises have participated. Of these, 1,550 have had their restructuring programs approved. However, the program is having difficulty reaching the small end of the SME sector, since these firms have problems in obtaining the required commercial bank sponsorship. They are too small for the commercial banks, and too large for the specialized micro credit bank.

Program effectiveness. About 1,550 enterprises benefited from the program, requiring total investment expenditures of Tunisian dinar (TD) 2.5 billion (US$1.8 billion) and matching incentives grants from the government of TD 356 million (US$260 million or 1.3 percent of GDP). These grants are funded by a 1 percent surcharge on the value added tax (VAT), which has raised, so far, about TD 30–40 million annually. In addition, the EU and the African Development Bank (AfDB) supported the program. The management of the *mise à niveau* concluded that, between 1997 and 2003, the firms benefiting from the program seem to have outperformed the manufacturing sector's benchmark with regard to turnover (11 percent growth, compared with 8.5 percent for the benchmark); export growth (16 percent growth, compared with 11 percent); and employment growth of 4 percent (not benchmarked). However, the real net effect of the *mise à niveau* program is not clear, either in terms of actual improved performance in relation to enterprises that have not benefited from such assistance, or in terms of penetration of export markets.

The mise à niveau program is controversial. While the EU and the AfDB are supporting the program financially, the Bank has reservations about its efficacy and the distorted incentives it encourages. The government feels that it would be politically very difficult to subject enterprises to more competition without supporting the enterprises with technical assistance and equipment financing to upgrade their operations. The government also seeks to support social stability through this program. The Bank's reluctance to support this program, given its reservations about the program's efficacy and the targeted nature of the support, is justified.

Source: OED mission findings.

World Bank Assistance Program

The World Bank has been a large player in Tunisia in both lending and policy influence. Annual average lending commitments for fiscal years 1990–03 were US$200 million (or US$20 per capita per year), representing over one-quarter of the MNA portfolio (figure 2.1). Annual average net disbursements were US$27 million; however, net transfers were negative for most of the period, as old loans were being serviced and repaid (the Bank has committed US$5.1 billion for 121 projects since 1958).

The Bank also served as a significant catalyst for mobilizing resources, leveraging US$1 on every IBRD (International Bank for Reconstruction and Development) dollar. The Bank also maintained an active policy dialogue, and its analytical work pointed out the agenda for reforms and guided Bank strategies and lending.

World Bank Assistance Strategies

In the 1990s and in 2000, World Bank programs were guided by country strategy documents (box 2.1). The overarching strategy objective is growth with equity. The Bank emphasized support for (i) stability and growth, boosting competitiveness, enhancing outward orientation, and rejuvenating private investment; (ii) human development; and (iii) rural development.

The mid-1990s country strategy was based on the 1995 Country Economic Memorandum (CEM), which argued for a Bank program in Tunisia that would support the country's efforts to promote economic integration within the world economy, and particularly that of the EU, while maintaining social stability and environmental sustainability (World Bank 1995a). The proposed Bank program under this country strategy emphasized nonlending services and, within lending operations, sector investment loans to support targeted sectoral policies to modernize key sectors (box 2.1).

The overarching strategy objective is growth with equity.

The 2000 Country Assistance Strategy (CAS) reaffirmed the main themes and objectives of its predecessor, reflecting the judgment that Bank assistance to Tunisia should stay the course of a strategy that had yielded good results so far and was still appropriate. Accordingly, the Bank would support Tunisia's efforts to increase its outward orientation, develop a larger and more dynamic private sector, further

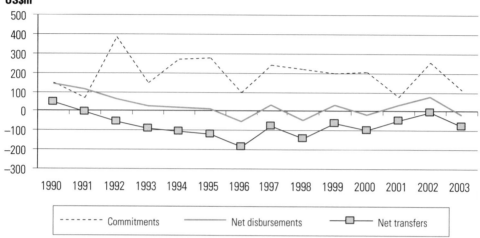

Figure 2.1 — Bank Commitments, Disbursements, and Transfers

strengthen human resources, and consolidate environmental management (box 2.1).

World Bank strategies were relevant and consonant with Tunisia's development priorities as outlined in a series of five-year plans. For example, the Ninth Development Plan (1997–00) aimed at opening up the economy to competition while maintaining macroeconomic stability and strengthening the social agenda and environmental management. The Tenth Development Plan (2002–06) also aims to strengthen competitiveness, embrace the knowledge economy, and meet the jobs challenge. The Bank strategies reflected Tunisia's development priorities as outlined in its development plans. The increased focus on the social sectors in the Bank strategies has been appropriate and is reasonably aligned with the MDGs and the country's emphasis on human resource development.

While largely relevant to Tunisia's development constraints and priorities, the country strategies did not pay sufficient attention to the fiscal sustainability of social policies.

While largely relevant to Tunisia's development constraints and priorities, the country strategies did not pay sufficient attention to the fiscal sustainability of social policies, with health care and social affairs absorbing a fifth of government spending,

and general education another fifth of the budget. There are serious education sector fiscal issues looming, with declining primary student populations and booming demand for secondary and higher education.

World Bank strategies developed indicators for monitoring results, but several of these are difficult to measure effectively since they are neither quantified nor time-bound. Many indicators exhibit such weaknesses as vague wording, input orientation, or no baseline data. For example, in the education sector, the 2000 CAS progress indicators include "greater cost recovery in higher education, improvements in teacher training"; and in the health sector, "enhance efficiency of public expenditure on health." Despite the declaration about the importance of monitoring and evaluation (M&E), the commitment to M&E is weak.[1] The 2000 CAS (p. 33) noted that the indicators were subject to refinements: "These indicators, to be refined with additional data availability, have been designed from available baseline values and reasonable medium-term targets."

Economic and Sector Work

Economic and sector work (ESW) was relevant, of high quality, conformed to the Bank's assistance strategy, and provided a solid basis for policy dialogue with the government (annex table A.4). Some core diagnostic ESW—

Box 2.1   World Bank Strategies

Mid-1990s Country Strategy: An Outward-Oriented Private-Sector-Led Growth Strategy

Goals. The objective was to promote rapid and sustainable outward-oriented and private-sector-based growth, while maintaining social stability and environmental sustainability. The strategy to achieve this objective emphasized: (i) deepening structural reforms to foster competition; (ii) human capital development toward middle-income standards; and (iii) modernization of key infrastructure services and environmental management.

Assistance program. Under the base case scenario, lending would average US$240 million per year during fiscal years 1996–99. The proposed program would allocate nearly half the portfolio to sectorwide investment loans, with the other half divided between policy-based loans and traditional investment projects. The base case scenario assumed satisfactory implementation of policy reforms and unavailability of other sources of finance (e.g., EU and AfDB). Triggers for higher lending levels (US$350 million per year) included a strong acceleration of structural reforms or a shock to the economy. The mid-1990s country strategy envisaged strategy notes on the role of the state and on structural changes in agriculture, and the general equilibrium model analysis of the impact of trade liberalization on the agricultural sector. In addition, the Bank would prepare a seminar on "Cross-Country Lessons from Civil Service Reform."

2000 CAS: An Update of the Earlier Strategy

Goals. The 2000 CAS substantially reiterated the mid-1990s country strategy objectives, noting that the pace of private investment remained gradual. The strategy to achieve these objectives was similar to that of the earlier period.

Assistance program. The CAS outlined three scenarios for the proposed lending program for fiscal years 2000–02. Under the base case scenario, the Bank would maintain the level of commitments of previous years, averaging about US$200 million per year. The proposed program would sustain the change in the mix of instruments begun with the mid-1990s country strategy, emphasizing sector investment loans, policy-based lending, and economic and sector work (ESW). The base case would include one policy-based operation (for US$150 million, or 25 percent) focusing on private sector development and/or the financial sector. Under the low-case program, lending would be scaled back, focusing on one or two investment-type operations targeted at the social sectors. Triggers for the high-case scenario included: (i) implementation of the free trade agreement with the EU, (ii) a substantial increase in privatization proceeds, (iii) further progress in financial sector reforms, and (iv) initiation of social security and labor market reforms. The level of commitments under the high case scenario was not proposed. Planned ESW included 18 reports, sector notes, and workshops covering trade, private sector development, social conditions, education, transport, water, and agriculture.

including the 1995 CEM, the 2000 Social and Structural Review, and the 1995 Poverty Alleviation report—covered macro, social, and sectoral issues and informed Bank strategies as discussed below. Other ESW sought to address known policy shortcomings in such sectors as finance and water, as well as labor and employment issues (annex table A.4). On the other hand, the last agricultural sector review was undertaken in 1982.

The World Bank's analytic and advisory activities (AAA) were generally sound but had some notable omissions, as discussed below. Tunisia is a relatively small country and increasing its integration into the global markets was appropriately emphasized; the high tariff and non-tariff barriers of the 1980s were distortionary, and replacing them with low and uniform tariffs was the right approach. The main thrust of the 1990 analytical work was to argue the case for a greater openness in the Tunisian economy in order to increase competition, and thereby the efficiency of investment. The work also emphasized the need to explicitly adopt a more aggressive export-orientation policy. The recommendations of a subsequent economic report in 1991 reinforced those of the earlier work and stressed the need to increase the efficiency of investment by increasing domestic and foreign competition.

Similarly, the Bank's analysis and its recommendations on private sector development and privatization were sound. The Bank economic work at the beginning of the 1990s emphasized the need to strengthen significantly the role of the private sector and to remove the barriers to domestic competition. The 1994 *Private Sector Assessment* also made a strong case for a relatively small country such as Tunisia to improve its export performance and, to that end, to significantly expand the role of the private sector (World Bank 1994b). That, the report argued, would in turn require policies to increase domestic and external competition and to remove obstacles facing the functioning of markets.

The 1995 CEM, *Republic of Tunisia: Towards the 21st Century*, built on the recommendations of these reports and underpinned the three strategic directions of the mid-1990s country strategy: (i) the pace of structural reform needed to move forward more decisively, particularly to complete trade liberalization and forcefully open up to private sector development; (ii) the State needed to redefine its role in the economy and concentrate on strengthening its role in the provision of public goods, while opening up much more significantly to the domestic and foreign private sectors; and (iii) despite good progress so far, the country needed to continue to upgrade human resources and environmental management to meet the expected increase in international competition. The CEM also included environmental considerations in its analysis of growth prospects and the role of government, and emphasized the need to assess the sustainability of land and water resources in an integrated fashion.

The 2000 *Social and Structural Review* (World Bank 2000b) and the 2000 *Private Sector Assessment Update* (World Bank 2000a) provided the main strategic orientation of the 2000 CAS. The review, which gave Tunisia high marks on economic reforms and achievement since the mid-1980s, argued that if the country hoped to achieve a level of development comparable to countries in the lowest tier of Organisation for Economic Co-operation and Development (OECD) countries, it needed not only to maintain reforms, but also to accelerate their pace, in view of the imminent

Despite strong growth, unemployment remains high, at around 15 percent.

threat of international competition in general, but particularly within the EU-related economic sphere. The *Update* represented another piece of good analysis that utilized a survey of Tunisian enterprises. It reiterated the main recommendations of the *Review*, presented a detailed review of private sector development to date, and made recommendations for future development.

During the first half of 2001, a sizeable Bank-Fund mission visited Tunisia twice, as part of the joint IMF-World Bank Financial Sector Assessment Program (FSAP). The overall assessment was that the authorities had implemented prudent and appropriate financial policies over the preceding decade, enabling the country to achieve reasonably high and stable growth with low inflation. A program to modernize, restructure, and consolidate banking, the securities market, and the insurance industry had been gradually implemented. It had so far included an overhaul of the legal and accounting frameworks, a strengthening of financial supervision, and a shift to more market-oriented policies. The assessment systematically examined the whole range of financial reform areas, pointing out where further action was needed and concluding with a list of policy priorities for the future.

Internal Bank analytical work tried to help the government understand why, despite strong growth, unemployment remains high, at around 15 percent. This work provided an in-depth analysis of the employment and labor market situation and made a number of recommendations to improve it. It concluded that unemployment remains high, partly reflecting demographic pressures, and partly the decrease in the employment intensity growth. While this analysis argued that the main solution to the employment problem is continued growth, it also provided an extensive list of recommendations to help improve employment policies and procedures to remove rigidities in the labor market, including facilitating exit of private firms.

The analytical reports were of satisfactory quality. The Quality Assurance Group (QAG) assessed a number of reports, rating them all either highly satisfactory or satisfactory. The recommendations were reflected in the 2000 CAS. Summary evaluations of key reports are provided in the forthcoming OED working papers (Kanaan; Tsakok) listed in the bibliography. Omissions in ESW include core diagnostic products: public expenditure reviews (PERs), Country Financial Accountability Assessments (CFAAs), and Country Procurement Assessment Reviews (CPARs). Periodic reviews of public expenditures would have been of particular importance to improving the efficiency and fiscal sustainability of social services, while at the same time preserving social gains.[2] Other fiduciary diagnostic reports—CFAAs and CPARs—are also essential to analyze issues related to economic management, governance, and transparency. Because of these omissions, the share of resources allocated to Tunisia's ESW—averaging 16 percent a year during the 1990s—was below the Bankwide average (18 percent), and far below the MNA average (21 percent) (annex table A.6).

Lending

The structure of the Bank's portfolio changed rapidly after 1990, when policy-based lending was introduced, with commitments amounting to nearly US$900 million (table 2.1). Economic policy, financial, and private sector development drew the largest amount of Bank support between FY90 and FY03 (39 percent of total Bank commitments), followed by education and health (21 percent), and rural/agriculture (19 percent). As evident from table 2.1, the Bank provided support to other sectors; however, this evaluation is confined to the above-mentioned sectors, constituting 80 percent of total commitments.

Resource mobilization. The Bank mobilized—in conjunction with various donor programs—a high co-financing ratio for its support. Between FY90 and FY03, the Bank attracted US$2,372 million in co-financing against US$2,745 million in IBRD commitments, leveraging nearly US$1.00 on every IBRD dollar (table 2.1).[3]

Table 2.1	Distribution of World Bank Commitments by Sector (FY90–03)					
Sector	**No. of Projects**	**Commitments**		**Co-financing**		
		US$m	**%**	**US$m**	**%**	
Economic policy, financial, and private sector development [a]	8	1,060	39	522	22	
Education	7	474	17	362	15	
Health, nutrition and population	3	106	4	108	5	
Rural [b]	10	525	19	787	33	
Energy and mining	1	60	2	39	2	
Environment	2	12	0	3	0	
Transport	3	139	5	87	4	
Urban development	4	250	9	401	17	
Water supply and sanitation	2	118	4	100	4	
TOTAL	**40**	**2,745**	**100**	**2,372**	**100**	
Memo items						
Adjustment	5	867	32	484	20	
Investment	35	1,878	68	1,888	80	

a. Includes ECAL I-III ($487 m), Economic and Financial Reform Support ($250 m), Public Enterprise Reform ($130 m), Export Development ($35 m), Industry Support ($39 m), and Private Investment Credit ($120 m).

b. Includes Northwest Mountainous and Forestry ($34 m) and Areas Development ($28 m), Agricultural Support Services ($21m), Water Sector Investment ($103 m), Agricultural Sector Investment I &II ($162 m), Natural Resource Management ($27 m), National Rural Finance ($65 m), Forestry Development II ($69 m), and Agricultural Research ($17 m).

Source: World Bank data as of September 30, 2002.

Table 2.2	IBRD Proposed and Actual Lending, FY97–02			
	Country strategy period FY97–99		Country strategy period FY00–02	
	Proposed	Actual	Proposed	Actual
Loan commitments				
(US$ million at current prices)				
Total during period	659	658	623	511
Average annual	220	219	208	170
(% of total commitments)				
Adjustment lending	25	36	25	49
Other	75	64	75	51

Source: Own calculations based on Bank's strategies.

The Bank's actual lending volumes were roughly the same as proposed in the CASs, but the share of adjustment lending was significantly higher than planned (table 2.2). Some projects included in the 2000 CAS base case were delayed due to low government interest or interventions by other donors, and others were reduced in scope.[4] The difference was made up by increasing the size of planned policy-based loans. Whereas the 2000 CAS base case called for one relatively small adjustment operation (US$150 million), the third Economic Competitiveness Adjustment Loan (ECAL III) was for US$253 million, or nearly half of the total lending program.

OED Findings on Closed Projects

OED ratings of Tunisia's projects have been high—in terms of outcome and sustainability—relative to all projects Bankwide and to other countries in the MNA Region (table 2.3). This is true for both adjustment and investment lending, while Tunisia's project rating in institutional development impact is similar to the Bankwide average.

Portfolio Performance Assessments

Ratings of Tunisia's project portfolio are also good and compare favorably with both MNA and Bankwide project ratings. Only 11 percent of Tunisia's active projects and 6 percent of commitments were considered "at risk." For

Table 2.3	OED Evaluation Findings of Recently Evaluated Projects by Value (exit since FY90)			
Country	Total evaluated (US$ million)	Satisfactory outcome (%)	Likely sustainability (%)	Substantial ID (%)
Tunisia	2,367	82	84	41
O/w adjustment lending	967	87	100	17
MNA Region	15,974	71	52	35
Algeria	3,253	46	721	
Egypt	2,025	83	40	34
Jordan	1,534	94	80	49
Morocco	4,736	67	38	59
Bankwide	251,234	76	66	43

Source: OED rating database, details in Annex A, table A5.

MNA as a whole, the comparable numbers are 25 percent and 28 percent; Bankwide, they are 18 percent for both projects and commitments. The Bank's current portfolio comprises 18 operations with commitments of over US$1.1 billion. About a third of the commitments are for financial and private sector development, another third for urban development and water supply (building new infrastructure and tourism development), a quarter for human development projects, and the remainder for transport and agriculture/rural development.

Efficiency of World Bank Assistance

The Tunisian country assistance program is relatively inexpensive (annex table A.6). The average program cost of US$13 per US$1,000 of net commitments for satisfactory and non-risky projects is lower than the MNA average of US$21 and the Bankwide average of US$16 for the 1990s. Tunisia's average project size is close to the Bankwide and MNA averages.

The Tunisian country assistance program is relatively inexpensive.

The Development Impact of World Bank Assistance

This chapter evaluates World Bank assistance by assessing its contribution to Tunisia's development outcomes. This is done by examining in more detail the progress in each of the three areas identified in the Bank's strategy: macroeconomic stabilization, growth, and structural reforms, including financial, trade, and private sector development; human resource development; and poverty alleviation and rural development.

Macroeconomic Stabilization, Growth, and Structural Reforms

The Bank's strategy has focused on maintenance of macroeconomic stability (in conjunction with the IMF) and promoting equitable and sustainable growth, mainly through increasing the country's openness to domestic and external competition. To promote increased competition, the Bank's assistance has been directed at a number of key structural areas, including financial sector reform, trade liberalization, enhancing the business environment, and promoting private sector development. All of the Bank's policy-based loans—the 1987 Industry and Trade Policy Adjustment Loan (ITPAL); the 1988 Structural Adjustment Loan (SAL); the 1991 Enterprise and Financial Reform Support Loan (EFRSL); and ECAL I (1996), ECAL II (1999), and ECAL III (2001)—have included the maintenance of a stable macroeconomic environment as a primary component and, therefore, have supported underlying fiscal, monetary, and exchange rate policies that have

been successfully implemented. As discussed below, they have also supported structural reforms in the financial, external, and private sectors. Tunisia's prudent macroeconomic management and cautious yet determined structural reforms have led to improved economic performance, essentially across the entire spectrum of standard indicators: sustained economic growth; declining inflation; a stable real exchange rate; a sound and stable fiscal position; controlled monetary aggregates; and a stable and manageable balance of payments position (table 1.2).

Real GDP growth accelerated from about 3 percent over 1986–90, to about 4 percent over 1991–95, and to over 5 percent over 1996–02, meeting the country strategy targets (annex table A.7a). Tunisia has been one of the fastest growing economies among MNA and other

Real GDP growth accelerated from about 3 percent over 1986–90, to about 4 percent over 1991–95, and to over 5 percent over 1996–02.

Table 3.1	Tunisia and Comparators: Per Capita Income Indicators					
	Tunisia		Lower-middle-income countries		MNA Region[c]	
Indicator	Mid-1980s[a]	Late 1990s[b]	Mid-1980s[a]	Late 1990s[b]	Mid-1980s[a]	Late 1990s[b]
GDP per capita ($ current)	1,158	2,137	1,422	1,665	2,852	2,512
GNP per capita ($ current)	1,160	2,060	1,250	1,740	1,990	2,000

a. Refers to data from 1982 to 1987.
b. Refers to data from 1994 to 1998.
c. MNA includes oil-exporting countries.
Source: World Bank (2000b).

lower-middle-income countries since the mid-1980s (table 3.1).

Financial Sector Reform

The Bank assistance program set out to decontrol interest rates, improve the soundness of the banking system, and privatize financial institutions. Next to stabilization policies, the reform and modernization of the financial sector has achieved the most progress. Certainly it has progressed more rapidly than other structural adjustment areas. The Bank and the Fund, among others, have been very active supporters in this area. Except for ECAL I, all the Bank adjustment operations had significant financial sector reform components, with ECAL II having been devoted entirely to that objective. The implementation experience of all these loans improved after a relatively slow start. The loans were based on analyses contained in several ESW pieces, including the 1995 CEM and the 2000 *Social and Structural Review*.

Initial progress was made in conjunction with ITPAL, with the partial freeing of interest rates, although ceilings were maintained for a number of sectors. A further initial and partial increase in competition was achieved in conjunction with the SAL, when certificates of deposit and commercial paper were introduced and a branch of a foreign bank was opened in Tunisia. Steps were also taken at that time to remove caps on interest rate spreads. In the early 1990s, and in conjunction with EFRSL,

The reform and modernization of the financial sector has achieved the most progress.

a new regulatory and supervision framework for banks was put in place; about 90 percent of interest rates were liberalized, although money market rates remained fixed by the Central Bank. The level of reform and Bank support in this sector were ratcheted up in the late 1990s in conjunction with ECAL II; all the agreed performance criteria for loan disbursement were met. The agreed targets for reducing nonperforming loans (NPLs) were also met, although at the expense of the budget and the banks. The overall soundness of the banking system improved significantly, in accordance with a number of prudential ratios. The activities of non-banking intermediaries increased appreciably, as did those of the securities and money markets. Civil code revisions regarding loan recovery were approved, although with some delay. A revised Banking Law that met international standards was submitted to the Chamber of Deputies, and a revised Civil and Commercial Procedures Code was approved.

Progress was made in privatization. An insurance company (Tunisian Lloyds) was privatized in conjunction with ECAL II. Most recently and in conjunction with ECAL III, another large insurance company (Al Ittihad) was restructured, and a new mutual fund company was created to take it over. The privatization of one commercial bank, *Union Internationale des Banques* (UIB), was completed and that of another, Banque du Sud, is proceeding, although at a pace that is slower than originally envisaged. In October 2002, the French group Société Générale bought a 52 percent stake in UIB. By 2002, assets in private banks were 55 percent of total bank assets, still below the 2000 CAS target of 60 percent (annex table A.7a). Eleven private leasing companies were operating in the country in 2001; leasing companies' share of financing private investment rose from 8 percent in 1996 to 12 percent in 2001.[1] At present, only four commercial banks remain in the public sector, with combined assets that represent 45 percent of the entire commercial banking system.[2] At least for the foreseeable future, there appears to be no intention to privatize these banks, because their continued role in the public domain is considered necessary to serve "strategic" sectors, one per sector: agriculture, housing, tourism, and micro-credit for very small enterprises (although there is talk of merging the last two). The government does not wish to relinquish the control it exerts over the bank and enterprises through the public banks, as it feels there is adequate competition since private banks are not prevented from operating in these sectors. Nevertheless, these public banks with their heavy burden of nonperforming loans pose risks to financial stability.

Progress in reform of the insurance industry, with much-appreciated World Bank support, has also taken place. Two insurance companies have recently been privatized; however, the country's largest insurance company, with a 34 percent share of the entire market, is likely to remain in the public sector for some time. As with the banks, the government is reluctant to give up ownership of some key entities that it uses to exercise control over part of the market or to provide subsidized services for social or stability reasons. But when the EUAA comes into effect in 2008, the Tunisian economy will have to align its structure along EU norms, which will require an even greater private role in the financial sector.

Nonperforming loans remain a top priority for action in the financial sector and for the economy at large. In conjunction with ECAL II, NPLs were reduced from about 36 percent in 1993 to about 19 percent in 2001,[3] which was still high. They are believed to have increased to 22 percent since 2002, reflecting the exposure of banks to the tourism sector, which was hit by the unfavorable

international environment. The Central Bank continues to closely monitor the situation and is implementing a scheme that allows it to work with the banks involved to clean up their portfolios over time. A major problem is that the judicial system is very slow in implementing procedures related to loan recovery; for example, the seizure of property used as collateral is possible in principle, but the procedure is so cumbersome and lengthy that it is effectively not an option that can be used at present. In addition to dealing with the stock of NPLs, it is even more important to deal with preventing new NPLs by addressing the root causes within the public enterprise (PE) sector (particularly the tourism sector). The Central Bank is trying to instill a new credit culture within the banking system to prevent new NPLs in the future.

The government is reluctant to give up ownership of some key entities that it uses to exercise control over part of the market.

Trade Liberalization

By the mid-1980s, Tunisia was a highly protected economy, with extensive restrictions on imports and a widely dispersed and high tariff structure. Immediately following the implementation of the successful stabilization in 1986, the country embarked on a number of structural reforms, including trade liberalization, to inject more competitiveness and efficiency into the economy. Both the Bank and the Fund gave priority to supporting the government program and often pressed it to take action in dismantling the quantitative restrictions (QR) regime and in reforming the tariff structure. Four Bank structural adjustment operations (ITPAL, SAL, EFRSL, and ECAL I) included trade liberalization components, and one investment operation (Export Development Project) supported export development through financing technical assistance and preshipment finance guarantees. Considerable analytical work was undertaken to support reforms in trade policy, including the 1994 report on the determinants of export growth (World Bank 1994a), the 1995 CEM, and the 2000 *Social and Structural Review*.

Early Bank operations with regard to dismantling the QR regime met with stiff resistance, and achieved only modest progress in rationalizing the tariff structure (e.g., the tariff range was compressed from 5–235 percent to 14–41 percent). This continued until the mid-1990s, when Tunisia joined the World Trade Organization (WTO) and signed the EUAA. On the eve of these events, 30 to 40 percent of imports were still subject to restrictions. Since then, liberalization has proceeded in the context of the free trade component of the EUAA. Tunisia's weighted average tariff rate fell from 30 percent in the mid-1990s to 27 percent in 2001. With the exception of Morocco's rate of 28 percent, Algeria, Egypt, and Jordan have lower rates (Annex table A-2l). Also, the weighted average tariff rate in non-MNA high-growth countries (Chile, Korea, Malaysia, Mauritius, and Thailand) is much lower, ranging from 5 percent in Malaysia to 16 percent in Mauritius.

Further progress in trade liberalization will be governed by implementation of the EUAA (i.e., full liberalization of the trade regime, at least regarding trade with the EU, is now expected in 2008). In the meantime, implementation of the early phase of the EUAA has actually increased effective protection, since duties on production inputs have been reduced ahead of those on final goods, but this is the standard nature of this agreement as applied in several other countries that have similar agreements with the EU. The gap between tariffs applied to imports from the EU and the rest of the world has also widened (annex table A-2m).[4] It would have been preferable for Tunisia to move more forcefully to lower protection and barriers to free trade. However, in view of the importance of the EUAA, it was understandable for the Bank to go along with the requirements of that agreement while pointing out the need for Tunisia to take other measures to enhance competitiveness, such as reducing cost of production. Such complementary measures have been slow in coming. In addition, the Bank could have helped design programs to reduce the discrimination against non-EU trade in parallel with implementation of the EUAA.

Private Sector Development and the Enabling Environment

Under the dirigiste system that characterized the economic structure until the mid-1980s, the economy was heavily regulated and public enterprises dominated the business sector, including banks and other financial intermediaries. Since 1987, the Bank has given top priority in its assistance strategy to helping the country inject more competition into the economy by creating a friendlier climate for private sector development, privatizing public enterprises, or helping them become more efficient. To that end, eight Bank lending operations (ASAL I [Agriculture Adjustment Loan], ITPAL, SAL, PERL [Public Enterprise Restructuring Loan], EFRSL, PICP [Private Investment Credit Project], ECAL I, and ECAL III) have included major components designed to help achieve these objectives. All these loans were, in turn, based on a set of high-quality ESW that included the 1994 and 2000 Private Sector Assessments and the 2000 *Social and Structural Review*.

The results and achievements of the country's efforts and the Bank's support have been mixed. Progress has been greatest in specific, more "technical" areas such as price decontrol and some aspects of the regulatory and procedural environment; progress on the more strategic dimensions such as the pace of privatization and addressing the financial and other problems of public enterprises has been slow but steady. For example, upon completion of the EFRSL in the early 1990s, prices and margins had been decontrolled for the bulk of commodities, although some controls remain to date at the retail level. A law prohibiting noncompetitive pricing was passed. A unified Investment Code was adopted under the EFRSL, although it still contained some costly and inefficient clauses such as tax privileges for foreign investors. A new Company Code was adopted in November 2002 and amendments are being proposed. Some modest measures have been implemented to facilitate labor mobility. A law that created a severance scheme for laying off workers has been passed, but enterprises continue to face obstacles and very

Figure 3.1 Business Climate Indices for Tunisia, MNA, and OECD (values 0–100)

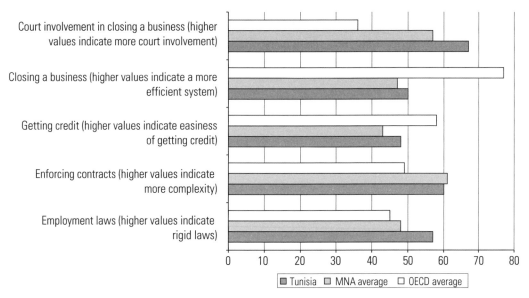

Source: Doing Business database (World Bank 2004).

complex procedures if they want to dismiss workers for "economic reasons."

Recent Bank surveys of the business climate show that the private sector enjoys a better business climate in Tunisia than in other MNA countries. Specifically, Tunisian entrepreneurs score higher, on average, than the entrepreneurs of other MNA countries in terms of starting a business, getting credit, and closing a business. In contrast, they face more rigid employment laws and more court involvement in the process of closing a business than the Regional average. Tunisia lags considerably behind the OECD countries (figure 3.1).

As far as privatization is concerned, 163 PEs were sold for a total of 2,345 million dinars (US$1720 million or 9 percent of GDP) during 1987–03 (table 3.2). When the privatization program started in 1987, the sectors earmarked for privatization were chosen strategically, but gradually other sectors of the economy were drawn in. The first privatization program (1987–94) targeted small and medium-size PEs, mainly in the textile, tourism, and construction sectors. The Bank supported the reform through a Public Enterprise Restructuring Loan

(PERL). However, the reform program was modest, resulting in the privatization of a few small-scale PEs, generating about US$80 million

The private sector enjoys a better business climate in Tunisia than in other MNA countries.

Table 3.2 Privatization by Sector, in Million Tunisian Dinar (1987 to August 31, 2003)

Sector	Total receipts	Of which: Receipts from foreign investors
Tourism	277	93
Transport	69	17
Chemical & mechanical industries	108	6
Trade	137	76
Agriculture, fishing, food	75	-
Construction materials	825	771
Textiles	19	5
Others	835	788
Total	2345	1756

Source: Ministry of Economic Development.

in sales proceeds. Further progress has taken place since 1995 with the privatization of large PEs—such as the cement plants—under ECAL I, with privatization proceeds amounting to US$570 million in 1998. Sales take place competitively primarily through invitations to tender with set terms and conditions, or through the securities market (annex table A.2j). However, in the recent privatization of Global System Mobile (GSM), the Bank was not comfortable with the process and allowed the associated floating tranche of ECAL III to lapse. Moreover, more information is needed on the relative importance of the privatized enterprises, in terms of their size in the PE sector and their contribution to employment, to assess the overall impact of the program.

Tunisia attracted a small but rising amount of foreign direct investment (FDI) inflows, averaging 2.6 percent of GDP, during the 1990s, compared with an average of 0.8 percent during the second half of the 1980s. Annual average FDI inflows to other MNA countries at similar income levels during the 1990s were also small: Jordan received an amount of FDI averaging 0.7 percent of GDP annually; Morocco, 1.1 percent of GDP; and Egypt, 1.1 percent of GDP (Dabour 2000).[5] Apart from small FDI amounts directed to tourism, Tunisia receives negligible FDI in the non-energy services sector (World Bank data, 2003).

In sum, a successful stabilization and economic growth program supported by the Bank and the Fund was maintained. Tunisia has also experienced a significant diversification of its resources, with non-oil/gas manufactures assuming a larger role in the economy. The Bank's program successfully promoted policy reforms in the trade, financial, and private sectors, especially with respect to improving the soundness of the banking system, as evidenced by a number of prudential ratios. Nevertheless, incomplete reforms in these areas have the potential to make it difficult to sustain past economic

The Bank's program successfully promoted policy reforms in the trade, financial, and private sectors, especially with respect to improving the soundness of the banking system.

performance, in light of the more competitive environment that Tunisia is likely to face in the next few years. Although tariffs have been reduced and the economy is now more open to the outside world, tariff rates are still high relative to competitors. Progress has been made in privatization, but it is not clear that the state's role in commercial sectors has been substantially reduced, because the Bank's program did not specify objective indicators for measuring progress, such as reducing the percentage of revenues or value added generated by state-controlled firms. Despite recent steps to eliminate past losses and establish a sound regulatory framework for the banking sector, nonperforming loans remain high and have risen recently, reflecting incomplete enterprise adjustment (e.g., privatization) and a slowdown in tourism. As a result, Tunisia's private investment remains low as a share of GDP (13.5 percent) and of total investment (56) and does not compare favorably with other MNA countries at similar income levels (annex table A.7a). Also, the private investment ratio to GDP in non-MNA high-growth countries (Chile, Korea, Malaysia, Mauritius, and Thailand) was 25 percent over the 1990s (World Bank data, 2003). Moreover, the country is already beginning to face some of the socioeconomic problems that prevail in more developed countries, such as persistent youth unemployment.[6] The Bank's program needs to continue to support Tunisia's effort to implement the EUAA and pursue trade openness beyond the EU, to improve the regulatory climate for private enterprises, to strengthen the court system to enforce business laws and regulations (particularly in relation to nonperforming loans), and to continue progress on enterprise and financial sector privatization.

Human Development and Progress toward MDGs

The Bank's human resource development strategy has emphasized achieving universal primary education, expanding post-primary enrollment, reducing infant mortality and fertility, increasing health coverage, and enhancing

Box 3.1	Tunisia's Progress in Meeting the Millennium Development Goals			
Indicator	**1990**	**1995**	**1999–2000**	**2015 Goals**
1. Eradicate extreme poverty and hunger	..	..	..	
Population below $1 a day (%)	..	2.0	..	1
Prevalence of child malnutrition (% of children under 5)	10.3	9.0	..	5.15
Income share held by lowest 20%	..	5.7	..	..
2. Achieve universal primary education				
Net primary enrollment ratio (% of relevant age group)	93.5	97.8	98.2	100
Youth literacy rate (% ages 15–24)	84.1	89.8	93.4	100
3. Promote gender equality				
Ratio of girls to boys in primary and secondary education (%)	81.9	89.1	93.0	100
Ratio of young literate females to males (% ages 15–24)	81.0	87.6	91.6	100
4. Reduce child mortality				
Under 5 mortality rate (per 1,000)	52.0	33.0	30.2	17.6
Infant mortality rate (per 1,000 live births)	37.3	30.5	25.8	12.3
Immunization, measles (% of children under 12 months)	93.0	91.0	84.0	..
5. Improve maternal health				
Maternal mortality ratio (modeled estimate, per 100,000 live births)	..	70.0	..	52.2
Births attended by skilled health staff (% of total)	80.0	81.0	82.0	..
6. Combat HIV/AIDS, malaria, and other diseases				
Prevalence of HIV, female (% ages 15–24)	..	..	..	a
Tuberculosis cases detected under DOTS (%)[b]	..	..	79.0	a
7. Ensure environmental sustainability				
Access to an improved water source (% of population)	80.0	..	..	90
Access to improved sanitation (% of population)	76.0	..	..	88
8. Develop a Global Partnership for Development				
Personal computer (per 1,000 people)	2.6	6.7	22.9	..
Fixed line and mobile telephones (per 1,000 people)	37.6	58.6	95.6	..

a. Halt and begin to reverse.

b. DOTS or "directly-observed treatment, short-course" is the internationally recommended TB control strategy.

Source: World Development Indicators database, April 2003.

the quality and efficiency of education and health services. The Bank's strategy focus on the social sectors is aligned with the MDGs and the country's emphasis on social achievements. With Bank and other donor support—for example, the EU, the African Development Bank (AfDB), and the French Development Agency (*Agence Française de Développement*, AFD)—Tunisia has already met some MDG target levels and is likely to meet them all by 2015 (box 3.1). The Bank's assistance contributed to many of these outcomes. Education and health were the basis for 21 percent of all Bank lending to Tunisia during the 1990s. Most of this went to education, a pattern repeated from previous decades.[7]

Education. The Bank focused initially on increasing enrollments, then shifted toward improving quality and efficiency. The consider- *Tunisia has already met some MDG target levels and is likely to meet them all by 2015.*

able Bank support to schools, vocational training, and more recently to universities, supplemented government resources substantially and also attracted a number of co-financiers. The government has assigned top priority to funding education ever since independence. At times, education accounted for over a quarter of the total budget of the central government—higher than in any comparator country, including those at much higher income levels. Much of the Bank's support and Tunisia's investment went into infrastructure and equipment, at times forming 85 to 90 percent of total project costs (annex table A.2o). Bank programs have been credited with improving basic education services, with particular emphasis on poor areas. Basic school enrollments have steadily risen to near 100 percent; between 1990 to 2001, there was a doubling in enrollment in the second cycle of basic and secondary schools (grades 7 to 12) (annex table A.7b).

Although early Bank education projects emphasized enrollment expansion, in line with government policy, the lending portfolio of the mid- to late 1990s addressed quality and efficiency. Recent projects have focused on teaching and learning processes that are child-centered and on improving the efficiency of education spending, albeit largely at the tertiary level. Repetition and dropout rates of sixth graders declined from 23 percent and 13.6 percent in 1995 to 8.1 percent and 4.7 percent in 2001, respectively.[8] Likewise, completion rates for grades 6 and 7 rose from 62 percent and 32 percent in 1995 to 87 percent and 63.5 percent in 2001, respectively (annex table A.7b). Basic, secondary, vocational, and tertiary facilities and services have also been enhanced, although further improvements are needed in the efficiency of services. For the vocational education subsector, attempts to improve the relevance of training and to strengthen linkages with the job market have been moderately successful.

Nevertheless, Bank projects have tended to equate quality with inputs (teacher training, class size, equipment, and higher spending per student) instead of student performance and outcomes. Weak monitoring and evaluation mechanisms helped sustain these assumptions and practices, and costs were not kept in check. Recent performance in international standardized testing (an outcome measurement) was poor, reinforcing concerns about the quality of education.[9] With Bank support, the government launched a reform program in 2002, including the introduction of new subjects (physics to students in the seventh grade and English to students in the fourth grade) and improvements in the quality of textbooks. However, funding of management and systemic improvements was small, even for those Bank projects with overridingly qualitative objectives.[10]

Areas that require closer monitoring by the government and warrant Bank support include expansion of the education system at the post-basic level, as demographic changes cause enrollment in basic education to fall and demand for secondary and higher education to increase (figure 3.2).[13] There are now 300,000 university students, and this number will rise to 500,000 by the end of the decade. The composition of education expenditure is more skewed toward the secondary and higher education levels than in other countries.[14] Public spending on education is already high (27 percent of total public expenditure and more than 7 percent of GDP in 2003), and cannot be expected to expand significantly, thus further improvements in efficiency need to be pursued. There is no mechanism for analyzing the education system's fiscal sustainability in the ongoing Bank-supported Education Quality Improvement Program Phase 1 (EQIP 1), which focuses on promoting inclusion in basic education by reducing dropout and repetition rates through improved teaching.[15] With the upcoming completion of the EUAA, the projected pressures on the budget for higher social spending, and the need to accelerate the reduction of the public debt by more ambitious fiscal consolidation, improving the efficiency of social expenditures is becoming of paramount importance.

Health. During interviews, government officials acknowledged the Bank's support for construc-

Figure 3.2 — Education System Expansion at the Post-Basic Level

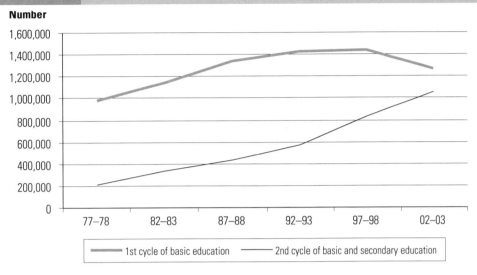

Number

1st cycle of basic education   2nd cycle of basic and secondary education

Source: Government data: Statistiques de l'enseignement scolaire.

tion of 20 percent of total primary health units and for providing equipment. Health coverage has expanded, and fertility and mortality have declined. The infant mortality rate dropped to 26 per thousand live births in 2002, compared with 30.5 in 1995, and total fertility rate declined to 2 biths per woman (table 1.4). The efficiency of large urban hospitals has improved with management upgrading and cost sharing with the social security program, and management information systems are being installed.[11] However, the Ministry of Health has not granted these hospitals the autonomy to fully manage their human resources and budgets.[12] Reform of health insurance has been slow. Recent reforms such as decentralization, regional health planning, and effective resource allocations are expected to enhance quality and efficiency.

In sum, the support of the Bank and other donors (EU, AfDB, and AFD) and the government's sustained emphasis on human resource development have resulted in remarkable progress in almost all areas covered by the MDGs (box 3.1). Figures 3.3–3.5 summarize the main achievements in comparison with the averages for MNA and other middle-income countries.

Poverty Alleviation and Rural Development[16]

Rapid economic growth laid the groundwork for poverty reduction, given that income inequality remained unchanged. The poor accounted for 4 percent of the population in 2000, down from 8 percent in 1990 (World Bank data). Tunisia's incidence of poverty is the lowest among MNA countries at similar income levels (annex tables A.2b and A.2c). Although rural poverty has decreased over the years, its 2000 level remained four times the urban level (World Bank data).

Controversy on poverty estimates not yet resolved. As mentioned earlier, there is a range of estimates of poverty in Tunisia. World Bank and Tunisian analysts note that poverty is predominately rural, and this contradicts the findings of the governmental institutions (Ayadi, Matoussi, and Feser 2001). Official Tunisian data shows that poverty has not been primarily rural since 1990. According to the National Institute of Statistics (INS), the incidence of rural poverty

Improving the efficiency of social expenditures is becoming of paramount importance.

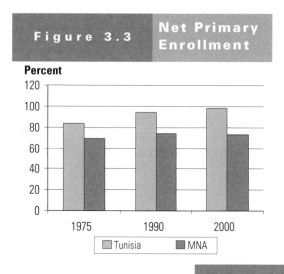

Figure 3.3 Net Primary Enrollment

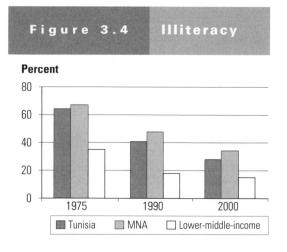

Figure 3.4 Illiteracy

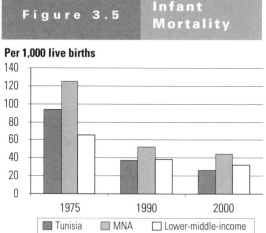

Figure 3.5 Infant Mortality

Source: World Bank, World Development Indicators database.

in 1990, 1995, and 2000 was 5.7, 4.9, and 2.9 percent, respectively. These levels are much lower than those reported by the Bank (table 1.3) (Tunisia 2000). The Bank is working with the Tunisian authorities to reconcile the methodological differences that are driving the substantial discrepancies in poverty estimates.

Every attempt should be made before the 2005 Household Survey and before the next poverty assessment is completed to address differences in poverty measurements.

It is important to close the large gap between estimates so that the focus can be shifted to policy and strategy to reduce poverty. Every attempt should be made before the 2005 Household Survey and before the next poverty

assessment is completed (a collaborative effort between the government and the Bank is recommended) to address differences in poverty measurements.

The Bank's rural development strategy. The Bank assistance strategies have broadly agreed on the following priorities for agriculture and rural development: (i) liberalize the agriculture sector, (ii) increase the efficiency of resource use, (iii) promote sustainable natural resource management, (iv) increase incomes in remote rural areas, (v) strengthen agricultural support services; and (vi) promote land consolidation and tenure security. These objectives have been rooted in the Bank's analytical work since 1982 (annex table A.4).[17] To achieve its objectives, the Bank provided a number of agricultural loans: two Agriculture Sector Adjustment Loans (ASALs), two Agriculture Sector Investment Loans (ASILs); one Water Sector Investment Project (WSIP); two Agriculture Research and Extension/cum/ Services projects; two Northwest Mountainous Areas Development Projects, one Forestry Development Project; one Natural Resource Management Project; and one Rural Finance Project. Progress toward addressing the Bank's program priorities is examined below.

Liberalization. With assistance from the Bank through the two ASALs, Tunisia has undertaken substantial agricultural policy reforms since 1989. Subsidies for fertilizer, animal feed, seed, irrigation, and mechanized services have been substantially reduced. The supply of farm inputs, collection of produce, and the provision of mechanized plowing and harvesting have been privatized. The role of private extension agents and veterinarians has expanded. Progress has been slower, however, in liberalizing food marketing, with the state remaining involved in cereals, milk, olive oil, sugar, tea, coffee, and tobacco.

Increased efficiency of resource use in irrigated perimeters. This objective, supported by ASIL and WSIP loans, was partially achieved as water tariffs were raised, and many water users' associations were created to manage irrigation in a decentralized way. Since Tunisia has not developed direct measurements of water savings at farm and irrigation perimeter levels, there is no direct measure. But there are some indirect measures, including the extent of the use of water-saving devices and the value added from the use of irrigated perimeters. In 1995, the government launched a national water savings program by subsidizing the purchase of water-saving equipment. So far, around 72 percent of the public irrigation perimeters are equipped with these devices. However, following the drought of 1998, the government started to subsidize water tariffs. This subsidization runs counter to the objective of increasing water tariffs and water-saving devices to improve efficient use. Regarding the value added from the use of irrigation perimeters, the continued subsidiza-

tion of wheat maintains an incentive system that favors the cultivation of cereals, a low-value crop. Problems of accessing the EU market[18] and domestic problems of marketing high-value crops are also undermining the switch to higher-value crops; addressing these problems warrants Bank support.

Sustainable natural resource management. There have been substantial physical achievements in Forestry II, Natural Resource Management, the Northwest Mountainous Areas, and the Northwest Mountainous and Forested Areas projects. For example, in the Northwest Mountainous Areas project the water conservation component was fully implemented, covering some 53,000 hectares. Improved soil management allowed farmers to plant pastures and alternative crops on land that would otherwise have been left fallow. An increased demand for agro-forestry species was met by the *Office du Développement Sylvo-Pastoral du Nord-Ouest* (ODESYPANO), a regional development agency, supporting the establishment of 36 small private enterprise nurseries. The Bank sought to improve natural resource management in a sustainable fashion by involving local communities. The partnership between the Forestry Department and local NGOs expanded from piloting 10 integrated rural development operations to 40. Forestry Groups with Collective Interest (*groupement forestier d'interet collectif*, GFIC), in forested areas, and Agricultural Development Groups (*groupement développement agricole*, GDA), in agricultural areas, have been created. The government subsequently allocated increased resources—budgetary and donor—to natural resource management.

Increased incomes in remote rural areas. The Bank sought to increase the incomes of poor farm families in remote rural areas such as the North West Region through its two Northwest Mountainous Area Development projects. It substantially achieved this objective as well as the broader objective of improving the living standards of these farm families (table 3.3). The major benefits to the poor have been improved

Table 3.3	Northwest Mountainous Areas Development Project: Selected Results from the 2000 Survey			
Indicator	**Unit**	**1996**	**2000**	**Difference (%)**
Agricultural income				
Less than 5 hectares	TD	1,113	1,633	46.7
More than 5 hectares	TD	3,141	4,724	50.4
Contribution to total household income				
Less than 5 hectares	%	47	48	1.0
More than 5 hectares	%	65	67	2.0
Employment on family farm	Work day	136	285	109
Distance to potable water	km	1.5	0.8	−46.7
Areas close to basic education facility	%	39	46	17.9
Distance from clinic	km	7	3.9	−44.3
Wheat yield				
Less than 5 hectares	QT/HA	11.5	13.6	18.3
More than 5 hectares		10.7	16.1	50.5
Barley yield	QT/HA	11.1	15.4	38.7

Notes: TD: Tunisian Dinar; km: kilometers; QT/HA: Quintal per hectare. 1 Quintal = 100 Kilos. The survey covered 158 households with less than 5 hectare farms and 101 households with greater than 5 hectare farms. These households come from 28 Community Development Groups.

Source: Northwest Forestry and Pastoral Development Agency (ODESYPANO).

The major benefits to the poor have been improved access to public goods and services, including schools, health facilities, and potable water.

access to public goods and services, including schools, health facilities, and potable water. The positive results on poverty reduction are supported by the Bank findings in 2003, which noted the overall reduction in rural poverty and pointed out that the North West Region is no longer the poorest of rural areas.[19] Table 3.3 also shows that farm income is only half of total household income for small farmers (with less than 5 hectares), reflecting the positive but limited contribution of improved agricultural techniques to rural vulnerability/poverty reduction. The project report points out that the very poor and landless did not benefit much from the agricultural interventions.[20] This highlights the need for supplementing efficiency gains with better-targeted safety nets.

Strengthen agricultural support services. The Bank sought to improve agricultural support services (such as research and extension and rural

finance) and to strengthen several institutions (such as water and community groups) as means to achieving developmental objectives. The outcome is mixed. The Bank achieved its objectives to improve participation and resource management and to increase family incomes by supporting water users associations and community development structures, both local-level institutions. The Bank's contribution to strengthening agriculture research and extension and rural finance to assist smallholders was less successful. Despite some progress, research and extension is far from being demand-oriented because the agendas of researchers still dominate, and the translation of research results into extendable messages is still problematic. In rural finance, government policy on debt forgiveness in response to drought continues to undermine financial discipline, and therefore the viability and reach of rural finance.

Land consolidation and tenure security. The Bank tried to promote land consolidation and tenure security as a means of improving incentives to invest in land and increase productivity, especially among smallholders. It succeeded in implementing some pilot cases, but did not succeed in accelerating the process of land consolidation and tenure security. A 2003 project performance assessment report (PPAR) notes that the Bank did not give sufficient attention to these complex and sensitive land issues and argues correctly that the Bank has largely tacked the land issue onto projects (ASAL II, ASIL I, and Northwest Mountainous Area projects) (World Bank 2003).[21] On the other hand, the Bank contributed in later years to raising government consciousness and increasing government resources for land issues.

To conclude, the Bank was successful in supporting measures that raised farm incomes in remote rural areas, increased local institutions' participation, and improved resource management sustainability. On the other hand, the Bank's contribution to linking research to extension, to enhancing rural finance, and to promoting land tenure and output markets was less successful. Future Bank programs should focus on these areas: supporting institutions essential for efficient functioning of output and input markets (for example, land and rural finance), while maintaining social cohesion through better-targeted safety nets for the rural population. Ministry of Agriculture (MOA) officials suggested that the Bank and the MOA should closely collaborate to undertake a sectorwide review as a first step. As MOA officials pointed out, the last agricultural sector review was carried out over 20 years ago, and a new review is needed to inform future Bank programs.

Outcome, Sustainability, and Institutional Development

The Bank's assistance, in tandem with that of the IMF and other donors, made a contribution to maintaining macroeconomic stabilization and structural reforms, which in turn facilitated growth. Along with sustained per capita income growth, solid progress was made in reducing poverty. With Bank assistance, the overall soundness of the banking system improved. However, large public banks with a heavy burden of nonperforming loans still dominate the banking sector and pose risks to the system's stability. Tariffs have been reduced and the economy is now more open to the outside world, but protection remains high compared with Tunisia's competitors. Further progress in trade liberalization will be governed by the implementation of the EUAA. The Bank's assistance also contributed to significant progress in the rural and social sectors. In the rural sector, the Bank's assistance made important contributions such as achieving sustainable resource use, increasing farm incomes, and improving living standards in remote areas. However, efforts to facilitate rural credit and land consolidation were less effective. With Bank support, remarkable progress in meeting the MDGs was made. Almost all children attend school, more children are surviving their first years, life expectancy has grown substantially, and gender equity has improved steadily. However, the Bank did not pay sufficient attention to the country's expanding social programs, and public expenditure reviews were not periodically undertaken. Overall, the outcome of the Bank's assistance program is rated satisfactory, based on its substantial relevance and efficacy.

There are two risks/vulnerabilities to sustainability: the relatively high level of external debt and large fiscal deficit increase Tunisia's vulnerabilities to external shocks, and vulnerabilities to regional and international developments, including the expiration of the MFA. However, the country has managed economic and regional political uncertainties quite well by gradually diversifying its export base, forging closer relations with the EU, and maintaining social and macroeconomic stability.[22] The progress achieved in attaining and maintaining macroeconomic stability is likely to be sustained—a broad political consensus that

Overall, the outcome of the Bank's assistance program is rated satisfactory, based on its substantial relevance and efficacy.

A broad political consensus that realizes the benefits and understands the importance of economic stability has evolved.

realizes the benefits and understands the importance of economic stability has evolved. Similarly, the structural reforms that have been accomplished have been based on a consensus among the key actors in the economy and are likely to be sustained. As Tunisia has joined WTO and has signed a free trade agreement with the EU, trade and investment policy reforms are unlikely to be reversed. Sustainability is rated likely.

The already relatively good institutional capacity in the country was strengthened further by the Bank's support. Institutional changes in Tunisia's policy, regulatory, and legal environment were accomplished with the help of Bank assistance. A broad range of investment, competition, and banking laws were implemented (annex table A.2n). New structures were established and now are operating successfully, such as the bank supervision and the associated revised banking law, and the new regulatory framework for mutual funds that complied with international standards and represented good progress in ensuring an adequate legal framework for the sector. On the other hand, there has been poor enforcement of regulations concerning loan recovery and, although a law that created a

severance scheme for laying off workers has been passed, enterprises continue to face obstacles and very complex procedures if they want to dismiss workers for "economic reasons."

Other organizations were restructured. The capacity of the ODESYPANO, a regional development agency in the northwest, still one of the poorest regions, and of the community development committees has been enhanced. Contracting of soil and water conservation works to private firms, privatization of veterinary services, and strengthening of water user and community development groups and agricultural development associations all have ahd a positive impact. On the other hand, the Bank's efforts to strengthen institutional development to promote rural finance, enhance research and extension, and address land tenure problems— some of the most difficult structural problems in rural development—had a limited impact. In contrast, substantial institutional and structural changes were made in the education and health sectors with the Bank's support, facilitating the remarkable progress toward meeting the MDGs. On average, the Bank's contribution to institutional development has been substantial.

Contributors' Performance

Tunisia's Own Central Role

The main party responsible for the significant socioeconomic achievements of Tunisia is the country itself. The Bank's support and that of other development partners no doubt played important roles, but it was the government's own belief in the correctness of the policies it followed and its ability to muster the national consensus to implement them that made the biggest difference.

Perhaps three main attributes of Tunisia's efforts were crucial for this overall success: (i) program ownership and the explicit policy of the government to move ahead with difficult policies and reforms only after a broad consensus with labor unions, the business community, and the political structure had been achieved, albeit within a regime that is governed by a strong central authority. Although this meant that the pace of reform had to be cautious and deliberate, it also meant that there have been no policy reversals and that economic agents could count on a basically predictable policy environment; (ii) the maintenance of high investment levels in human resources, which has led to a well-educated population and a well-trained and qualified labor force; and (iii) the achievement and maintenance of macroeconomic stability through a combination of sound fiscal, monetary, and foreign exchange policies.

These factors enabled the country to implement reforms across a wide variety of areas: price liberalization, trade, financial and private sector development, investment incentives, legal and institutional frameworks, human resources, and agriculture and rural development. However, although comprehensive, both the pace and the depth of reforms have been uneven. Whereas stabilization policies were implemented rather swiftly and generally have been maintained, and broad fiscal and financial sector reforms have moved forward rapidly, progress with public enterprise restructuring and privatization has been relatively modest, proceeding at a more cautious pace because

The main attributes of Tunisia's success were ownership and broad political consensus, a well-developed human resource base, and a stable macroeconomic environment.

the consensus behind them is not as firm. In addition, labor mobility remains hampered by rigidities in the labor market, whose removal has experienced considerable resistance from the unions. Trade liberalization, on the other hand, was initially resisted and had moved slowly, but eventually would accelerate under the EUAA free trade agreement. The government has placed strong emphasis on education. This investment has paid off impressively: rising education standards were a major contribution to the rise in total factor productivity.

According to some policymakers, the 1986–93 period represented the first phase of reforms that were not fully developed at the time and, sometimes, not fully owned by the country. This led to mixed and partial results and some slippage in implementing policies. To these practitioners, 1993 signaled the beginning of the "post-adjustment" phase, in preparation for the signing of the EUAA in 1995. During this period, the authorities took a couple of years to develop their own program and build the requisite internal consensus for its support. This served as the basis for the three Economic Competitive Adjustment Loans (Tunisian officials chose the name over a Structural Adjustment Loan [SAL], noting that adjustment had already been completed and the country had entered its post-adjustment phase). However, even when the authorities have themselves been convinced of the reforms that they owned, they have chosen to continue to move prudently and deliberately to ensure that all concerned were on board. In the words of an official, "We wait until things ripen and then we move, step-by-step. This is why there have been no reversals or slippages in this phase. For example, after seven years of partial trade liberalization and five years of hesitant privatization, both have now accelerated."

In the words of an official, "We wait until things ripen and then we move, step-by-step. This is why there have been no reversals or slippages."

Perhaps the most controversial issue has to do with the "appropriate" pace of reform. The gradualist, cautious approach followed by the Tunisian authorities to ensure as broad a political consensus as possible in sensitive areas has led to some delays, from the standpoint of the Bank, and it entails some risks, as the economy faces growing competitive pressures. But on the other hand, the gradual approach has allowed the government to build the necessary consensus and has served the overall objective of reform well, at least so far. Bank staff went along with this pace in general, but by the late 1990s started encouraging Tunisia with more urgency to accelerate the implementation of its reforms and make the private sector more open and transparent, in view of the significant increase in competitive pressures expected for the country. Because of domestic opposition to the more difficult measures required, the Tunisians have elected not to abandon the gradualist approach that has served them well so far, in order to avoid risking a major derailment of reforms.

The World Bank's Performance

The Bank provided significant assistance to support the country's development efforts. Its analytical work was timely; the topics covered were driven by socioeconomic developments in the country. It was generally of high quality and important for the design of the Bank's strategies. It also underpinned the Bank's lending.

Policy-based and sector investment loans were generally well conceived and designed.[1] They covered the right policy areas, starting with a broad catch-all operation such as the Industrial Trade Policy and Adjustment Loans, which were appropriate for the early days of reform, and became more focused and specific as the process matured. Successive operations covered the same set of areas, but each time building on previous progress and adding new and deeper dimensions. This reasonable approach worked particularly well in financial reform, where Bank assistance supported the country first in introducing the basic rudiments of a modern financial system in the early days, and then in adopting more specific measures appropriate for a more advanced system by the turn of the century. Similarly, early education and health projects placed more emphasis on improving access; the lending portfolio of the later 1990s was more focused on sectorwide policy issues such as enhancing the quality of services.

In general, Bank staff and management showed reasonable flexibility during implementation. For example, Bank staff showed flexibility during ECAL I preparation, reaching an agreement with the government to postpone the banking reforms initially envisaged in the operation in order to arrive subsequently at a fully agreed policy package for the sector loan (ECAL II). This flexibility entailed a reduction of the ECAL I amount by half. On the other hand, the Bank was not comfortable with the telecommunication privatization process, and decided to allow the floating tranche of ECAL III to lapse. In a few instances, a technical or partial waiver for a tranche-release condition had to be given, or a loan covenant was not honored, and the Bank still disbursed the loan. This was normally a negotiable approach, since the agreed measures were subsequently implemented and the momentum of the overall reform effort maintained.

In particular, an explicit approach of "incremental progress" by all the parties involved has proven very effective in Tunisia. This approach involved the Bank staying the course in a particular policy area and addressing the same or closely related issues in that policy area with successive analytical pieces or lending operations, but each time incrementally and patiently introducing additional measures until more complete progress was achieved over time. This was particularly clear in the more difficult areas in finance, agriculture, and investment incentives—areas where political resistance initially slowed down the rate of progress, and patience and persistence proved worthwhile.

As is to be expected, where there was strong concordance between the Bank and the government (as in the case of the Natural Resource Management Project), there was great progress, and vice versa, as in the case of rural finance. The Bank was not able to change the government's traditional approach of rescheduling and forgiving debts as a method of drought relief. This behavior undermined incentives to repay the National Agricultural Bank (*Banque Nationale Agricole* or BNA) loans, even among farmers in irrigated areas who were not drought-afflicted.

While turnover of country directors for Tunisia has not been high (annex table A.9), staff rotation is relatively high at the project level. There have been 3 or more task managers in 8 (24 percent) out of 33 projects (annex table A.8). The turnover was the highest for the Hospital Restructuring Loan, which had five task managers, and the Private Investment Credit, which had four. Ongoing projects with a high turnover of task managers include the Education Quality Improvement Program (with three task managers).

As is to be expected, where there was strong concordance between the Bank and the government, there was great progress, and vice versa.

Other Development Partners

The International Monetary Fund. Tunisia joined the Fund in April 1958. The IMF has played a significant role in supporting the country's successful stabilization and financial sector reform efforts. As with the Bank, the Fund provided valuable technical advice and considerable funding and played an important role in helping the government avert the threatening balance of payments crisis in the mid-1980s. A Standby Arrangement in an amount of SDR 103.65 million was approved in July 1988, and a drawing of SDR 207.30 from the Extended Fund Facility was approved in July 1992. These amounts were very important in helping Tunisia meet external financing requirements, and the underlying programs supported the government's efforts to maintain macroeconomic stability and implement structural reforms in a number of the areas also supported by Bank adjustment lending. The Fund and the Bank jointly conducted a financial assessment. The Fund also provided assessments of the country's macroeconomic conditions under the three ECALs. The Fund and the Bank also cooperated in a number of areas to provide technical advice, most

An explicit approach of "incremental progress" by all the parties involved has proven very effective in Tunisia.

notably for the financial sector and debt management.

The European Union. The partnership between Tunisia and the EU has been very strong, both with the Commission itself and with the European Investment Bank (EIB). Over the 1977–96 period, four financial protocols were implemented, for a total support from the European Union of euro 742 million; of this, euro 324 million is directly from the Commission's budget, and euro 418 million is from the EIB. Priority was given during this period to support agriculture and rural development, environmental management, transport, industry, infrastructure, and training. After Tunisia signed the Association Agreement in 1995, the nature of the support shifted significantly under the MEDA I program (1996–99). In line with the Tunisian government's priorities at the time, 48 percent of this program's euro 428.4 million support was for structural adjustment, in conjunction with World Bank ECAL support. In addition, the EIB provided euro 620 million in loans, mainly in support of infrastructure, environmental protection, and private sector development. MEDA II (2000–06) was designed to support similar priorities that were further emphasized in the *Document de Strategie (2002–2006)* and the accompanying *Pro-gramme Indicatif National (2002–2004)*. Under MEDA II, the Commission provided euro 249 million for structural adjustment; modernization of industry, the judiciary, ports, and information technology; the media; and greater participation of civil society in socioeconomic development. The EU analyses of economic developments and prospects in Tunisia are similar to the Bank's. They give the country high marks on macroeconomic stabilization and good overall performance on structural adjustment, but stress the need to accelerate the implementation of policies that would increase competitiveness, such as further export-orientation, private sector development, and dealing more decisively with the public enterprise sector through the *mise á niveau* (box 1.1) program. Finally, the EU has also given Tunisia high marks for its efficient absorptive capacity of the EU assistance program.

The EU has co-financed all three Bank-supported ECALs, for a total of euro 260 million. The EU—along with the German Agency for Reconstruction (*Kreditanstalt für Wiederaufbau,* or KfW) and AFD—has been an important partner in the Bank's rural development program. Staff of the EU delegation in Tunis feel that the cooperation with the Bank has basically been very good, especially during loan preparation and appraisal, but that the Bank could do a better job of actively engaging EU staff during loan implementation and supervision. The EU noted the lack of Bank representation in Tunis. At present, the Bank has only a liaison office in Tunis, staffed by one Operations Officer; the Country Director is based in Washington, D.C.

The African Development Bank. AfDB has enjoyed excellent cooperation with Tunisia and has contributed significantly to its development effort. Since the beginning of its operations in the country in 1968, it has committed about US$4,290 million equivalent in support of 84 operations. AfDB loan commitments have averaged about US$250 million equivalent annually in recent years. These loans have given priority to electrification, roads, railways, water resources, agriculture, rural development, and structural adjustment, in conjunction with the three ECALs (for a total of about 330 million AfDB currency units), and small and medium-size enterprise (SME) development through support of the *mise á niveau* program in conjunction with the EU. AfDB staff working on the ECALs commended the excellent working relationship with the Bank.

The Islamic Development Bank. Tunisia joined the IDB in 1974, and since then has enjoyed an exemplary relationship with the IDB. The IDB supported Tunisia's development efforts by providing trade financing (US$818 million), project financing (US$355 million), and special assistance (US$4 million). Priorities for IDB assistance have been public utilities, mainly water and sewerage (44 percent), agriculture and integrated rural development (17 percent), and social sectors (15 percent). The IDB co-financed one World Bank project and the working relationship between the two institutions has been excellent.

Exogenous Factors

The amount of rainfall in a particular year is a very important, unpredictable, and ever-present exogenous factor for Tunisia. It has an immediate effect on agricultural production, which, because of its significant share of GDP, greatly influences aggregate production. The cyclical nature of GDP in Tunisia is the product of rainfall cycles, and it is interesting to note in this context that this cyclical relationship is asymmetric. The influence of agricultural production on GDP is stronger in the contraction phase than in the expansion phase, since when agricultural output is higher than normal, its multiplier effect through its use by agro-industries takes place only if spare capacity is available. There is also a household incomes effect that reinforces this asymmetry.

Another important exogenous factor that applies to most countries is the level of economic activity in trading countries. In the case of Tunisia, this means essentially the rate of economic growth in the EU. Because of increasing international competition in exports to the EU, this factor is likely to be quite significant, particularly during years of low or negative EU growth.

Although Tunisia is not a direct participant in the Middle East conflict, its economy can still feel any significant perturbations in the region, as happened during the Gulf War; the attack in Djerba, a tourist resort; and the current uncertain situation in Iraq.

By their nature, exogenous factors are not within the country's control. But Tunisia can try to build up resilience against them by increasing the flexibility of its economic structure so it can respond more rapidly to unpredictable changes in its environment. Its prudent macroeconomic stabilization measures and adjustment program to make the economy more open and competitive have enabled Tunisia to weather some of these factors over the past couple of decades.

The amount of rainfall in a particular year is a very important, unpredictable, and ever-present exogenous factor for Tunisia.

Recommendations

This evaluation finds that a combination of macroeconomic stability, attention to human resource development, and structural reform can yield dramatic improvements in the living standards of developing countries. Also, government ownership of reforms and the reform program are important ingredients of a successful Bank assistance program. It also shows that ESW can play an important role in formulating and supporting reform programs that underline Bank lending, particularly adjustment lending. In this regard, omission of diagnostic work, such as sector work, public expenditure analysis, and core fiduciary work do have an impact on the Bank's programs in sectoral reform, the efficiency of public expenditures, and accountability.

This evaluation has the following recommendations:

- *Follow through on supporting programs to improve the environment for private sector development and enhance competitiveness,* as Tunisia seeks to integrate within the world economy. Specifically, the Bank should help the country (i) pursue trade openness with the EU and the rest of the world; (ii) improve the enabling environment to attract private and foreign investment; (iii) strengthen the judicial system to implement laws and regulations regarding loans recovery, particularly nonperforming loans and measures to facilitate exit of private firms; and (iv) continue progress on privatizing public financial and enterprise firms.

- *Continue support for social sectors.* While supportive of the MDGs, the Bank's program needs to continue this emphasis and focus on improving the country's capacity to prioritize public spending and address burgeoning demand for secondary and tertiary education—given the demographic transition under way—while preserving social gains. As expenditures on social services remain high, representing over 40 percent of expenditures, education expansion at the post-basic level will necessitate efficiency improvements. A public expenditure review could help build capacity to prioritize social spending and provide the basis for measures to efficiently address education expansion.

- *Focus on institutional development and safety nets in the rural sector.* Future Bank programs should focus on institutional development to support efficient output and input markets (for example, land and rural finance), while maintaining social and political stability through better targeted rural safety nets. Good quality economic and sector studies should inform future Bank programs. After 21 years without a comprehensive Bank agricultural sector review, OED agrees with the government's suggestion that it is time to undertake one.

- *Enhance a results-based monitoring and evaluation approach.* Strengthening monitoring of output and outcome indicators embedded in an improved monitoring and evaluation function would help to anchor the Bank's future assistance program in a result-based approach.

ANNEXES

ANNEX A: STATISTICAL ANNEXES

Annex A.1   Tunisia at a Glance

POVERTY and SOCIAL	Tunisia	M. East and North Africa	Lower-middle-income
2002			
Population, mid-year *(millions)*	9.8	306	2,411
GNI per capita *(Atlas method, US$)*	2,000	2,070	1,390
GNI *(Atlas method, US$ billions)*	19.6	670	3,352
Average annual growth, 1996–02			
Population *(%)*	1.2	1.9	1.0
Labor force *(%)*	2.4	2.9	1.2
Most recent estimate (latest year available, 1996–02)			
Poverty *(% of population below national poverty line)*	..	..	..
Urban population *(% of total population)*	67	58	49
Life expectancy at birth *(years)*	73	69	69
Infant mortality *(per 1,000 live births)*	24	37	30
Child malnutrition *(% of children under 5)*	4	..	11
Access to an improved water source *(% of population)*	80	88	81
Illiteracy *(% of population age 15+)*	27	35	13
Gross primary enrollment *(% of school-age population)*	117	95	111
Male	120	98	111
Female	115	90	110

KEY ECONOMIC RATIOS and LONG-TERM TRENDS	1982	1992	2001	2002
GDP *(US$ billions)*	8.1	15.5	20.0	21.2
Gross domestic investment/GDP	31.7	34.3	27.9	25.8
Exports of goods and services/GDP	36.9	39.5	47.1	44.3
Gross domestic savings/GDP	21.2	27.4	23.4	21.4
Gross national savings/GDP	22.5	26.4	23.6	22.4
Current account balance/GDP	−9.2	−7.0	−4.3	−3.5
Interest payments/GDP	2.7	2.6	2.1	2.2
Total debt/GDP	46.4	56.1	54.5	57.2
Total debt service/exports	16.2	20.0	13.9	15.4
Present value of debt/GDP	..	..	54.2	..
Present value of debt/exports	..	..	102.7	..

	1982–92	1992–02	2001	2002	2002–06
(average annual growth)					
GDP	3.8	4.7	4.9	1.7	4.7
GDP per capita	1.3	3.2	3.7	0.5	3.7
Exports of goods and services	7.2	5.6	12.1	0.0	5.5

STRUCTURE of the ECONOMY	1982	1992	2001	2002
(% of GDP)				
Agriculture	13.2	16.1	11.6	10.4
Industry	31.1	28.5	28.8	29.1
Manufacturing	11.1	16.5	18.5	18.6
Services	55.8	55.4	59.5	60.5
Private consumption	62.3	56.6	60.9	62.3
General government consumption	16.5	16.0	15.7	16.3
Imports of goods and services	47.4	46.5	51.7	48.7

	1982–92	1992–02	2001	2002
(average annual growth)				
Agriculture	5.3	1.9	−1.5	−10.3
Industry	3.6	4.8	5.7	3.4
Manufacturing	2.0	5.6	6.9	2.2
Services	3.4	5.3	6.0	3.7
Private consumption	2.7	4.6	5.4	3.4
General government consumption	3.0	4.2	5.0	4.5
Gross domestic investment	0.8	3.7	6.4	−6.2
Imports of goods and services	3.0	4.7	13.4	−1.7

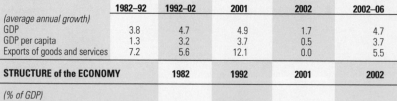

Development Diamond*

Life expectancy

GNI per capita — Gross primary enrollment

Access to improved water source

—— Tunisia
—— Lower-middle-income group

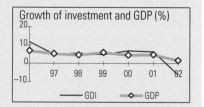

Economic ratios*

Trade

Domestic savings — Investment

Indebtedness

—— Tunisia
—— Lower-middle-income group

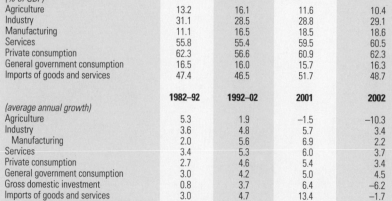

Growth of investment and GDP (%)

—— GDI   —◇— GDP

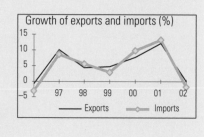

Growth of exports and imports (%)

—— Exports   —◇— Imports

Note: 2002 data are preliminary estimates.
This table was produced from the Development Economics central database.
* The diamonds show four key indicators in the country (in bold) compared with its income-group average. If data are missing, the diamond will be incomplete.

PRICES and GOVERNMENT FINANCE	1982	1992	2001	2002
Domestic prices (% change)				
Consumer prices	..	5.8	1.9	2.8
Implicit GDP deflator	16.0	5.7	2.7	2.8
Government finance				
(% of GDP, includes current grants)				
Current revenue	31.7	26.8	24.6	24.6
Current budget balance	6.7	4.1	5.2	4.7
Overall surplus/deficit	−2.2	−3.0	−3.5	−3.1

TRADE	1982	1992	2001	2002
(US$ millions)				
Total exports (fob)	1,980	4,014	6,606	6,857
n.a.	911	609	610	641
n.a.	63	416	541	489
Manufactures	965	2,432	4,981	5,272
Total imports (cif)	3,389	6,432	9,521	9,503
Food	356	430	654	653
Fuel and energy	377	449	888	886
Capital goods	1,032	1,578	2,240	2,236
Export price index (1995=100)	..	79	151	154
Import price index (1995=100)	..	89	107	109
Terms of trade (1995=100)	..	89	141	141

BALANCE of PAYMENTS	1982	1992	2001	2002
(US$ millions)				
Exports of goods and services	3,002	5,973	9,518	9,539
Imports of goods and services	3,859	6,978	10,423	10,431
Resource balance	−856	−1,005	−905	−893
Net income	−294	−654	−941	−984
Net current transfers	403	570	983	1,130
Current account balance	−748	−1,089	−863	−746
Financing items (net)	776	1,171	1,118	895
Changes in net reserves	−27	−82	−255	−149
Memo:				
Reserves including gold (US$ millions)	614	862	1,999	2,301
Conversion rate (DEC, local/US$)	0.6	0.9	1.4	1.4

EXTERNAL DEBT and RESOURCE FLOWS	1982	1992	2001	2002
(US$ millions)				
Total debt outstanding and disbursed	3,772	8,543	10,884	12,100
IBRD	376	1,470	1,297	1,464
IDA	68	56	37	35
Total debt service	563	1,342	1,465	1,641
IBRD	53	267	226	233
IDA	1	2	2	2
Composition of net resource flows				
Official grants	29	140	..	..
Official creditors	279	278	365	−90
Private creditors	29	74	229	556
Foreign direct investment	340	526	..	..
Portfolio equity	0	0	0	..
World Bank program				
Commitments	0	210	328	112
Disbursements	83	111	293	117
Principal repayments	27	149	148	156
Net flows	56	−39	145	−39
Interest payments	27	120	80	79
Net transfers	29	−159	65	−118

Note: This table was produced from the Development Economics central database.

Inflation (%)

Export and import levels (US$ mill.)

Current account balance to GDP (%)

Composition of 2001 debt (US$ mill.)

A - IBRD
B - IDA D - Other multilateral
C - IMF
E - Bilateral
F - Private
G - Short-term

ANNEX A.2:   KEY BACKGROUND DATA

Table A.2a	Tunisia: Key Economic and Social Indicators, 1990–01						
Indicator	**1990**	**1991**	**1992**	**1993**	**1994**	**1995**	**1996**
GDP growth (annual %)	8.0	3.9	7.8	2.2	3.3	2.3	7.1
GNI per capita, Atlas method (current US$)	1,430	1,490	1,700	1,690	1,740	1,820	2,000
GNI per capita, PPP (current international $)	3,770	3,940	4,310	4,400	4,540	4,720	5,030
GDP per capita growth (annual %)	5.4	1.9	5.6	0.2	1.4	0.7	5.5
Agriculture, value added (% of GDP)	15.7	16.7	16.1	14.7	12.6	11.4	13.7
Manufacturing, value added (% of GDP)	16.9	16.9	16.5	17.1	18.3	18.8	18.3
Services, etc., value added (% of GDP)	54.5	54.3	55.4	57.3	58.4	59.6	57.8
Exports of goods and services (% of GDP)	43.6	40.4	39.5	40.4	44.9	44.7	42.1
Imports of goods and services (% of GDP)	50.6	45.3	46.5	48.0	47.9	48.7	43.7
Current account balance (% of GDP)	−3.8	−3.6	−7.1	−9.1	−3.4	−4.3	−2.4
Total debt service (% of GNI)	26.7	26.0	21.9	22.9	20.8	18.4	17.8
External debt, total (% of GNI)	64.7	65.7	57.8	63.2	65.2	62.1	59.7
Gross foreign reserves in months of imports	1.6	1.6	1.4	1.4	2.2	2.5	3.1
Current revenue, excluding grants (% of GDP)	30.7	29.0	29.4	30.3	31.3	30.1	29.6
Expenditure, total (% of GDP)	34.6	34.0	32.1	33.1	32.3	32.8	32.6
Gross domestic savings (% of GDP)	25.5	27.1	27.4	21.7	21.5	20.7	23.5
Illiteracy rate, adult total (% of people ages 15 and above)	40.9	39.8	38.7	37.7	36.5	35.3	34.1
Immunization, DPT (% of children under 12 months)	93.0	93.0	95.0	94.0	93.0	94.0	95.0
Improved water source (% of population with access)	80.0	..	..	..	..	..	..
Improved sanitation facilities (% of population with access)	76.0	..	..	..	..	..	..
School enrollment, primary (% gross)	113.3	113.7	114.1	116.6	117.2	116.8	116.5
School enrollment, secondary (% gross)	44.9	45.9	48.6	53.2	56.8	60.4	64.6
Population, total (in millions)	8.2	8.3	8.5	8.7	8.8	9.0	9.1
Population growth (annual %)	2.4	2.0	2.0	2.0	1.8	1.6	1.5
Urban population (% of total)	57.9	58.7	59.5	60.3	61.1	61.9	62.6
Life expectancy at birth, total (years)	70.3	70.5	70.8	70.8	71.0	71.4	71.6
Fertility rate, total (births per woman)	3.5	..	3.2	..	2.9	2.7	2.5
Infant mortality rate (per 1,000 live births)	37.3	35.7	34.2	32.3	31.7	30.5	29.7
School enrollment, primary, male (% gross)	119.6	119.5	119.4	121.6	121.8	120.9	120.1
School enrollment, primary, female (% gross)	106.6	107.5	108.6	111.4	112.4	112.6	112.6
Illiteracy rate, adult male (% of males ages 15 and above)	28.4	27.6	26.7	26.0	25.0	24.0	23.0
Illiteracy rate, adult female (% of females ages 15 and above)	53.5	52.1	50.8	49.4	48.1	46.7	45.3

Source: World Bank database as of March 23, 2003.

| 1997 | 1998 | 1999 | 2000 | 2001 | Average, 1990–2000 | | | | | | |
					Tunisia	Algeria	Egypt	Jordan	Morocco	MNA	Lower-middle-income countries
5.4	4.8	6.1	4.7	5.4	4.7	2.0	4.6	4.8	4.8	3.0	3.7
2,080	2,050	2,090	2,100	2,070	1,855	1,741	1,086	1,513	1,162	1,876	1,100
5,220	5,350	5,730	6,070	6,450	4,961	4,591	3,039	3,628	3,188	4,595	3,824
4.0	3.4	4.7	3.5	4.2	3.1	0.1	2.6	0.9	0.9	0.9	2.5
13.2	12.5	12.9	12.3	11.8	13.6	11.1	17.3	4.7	16.5	14.0	15.3
18.5	18.4	17.9	18.2	18.1	17.8	10.8	17.8	14.7	17.6	13.1	25.9
58.2	59.2	59.2	58.9	59.4	57.7	35.9	50.5	68.8	51.6	46.2	45.3
43.8	43.0	42.2	44.0	44.2	42.7	28.8	21.2	49.5	27.4	31.8	27.2
46.2	46.3	44.4	47.6	47.8	46.9	24.7	27.8	74.2	32.7	31.6	26.6
−3.1	−3.4	−2.2	−4.2	−4.7	−4.3	3.7	1.3	−4.7	−1.3	..	..
17.1	16.8	17.3	22.2	..	20.7	49.4	18.9	22.8	37.3	16.8	15.2
60.7	56.7	60.1	59.7	60.2	61.5	63.9	55.7	142.3	71.6	41.3	36.6
3.1	2.6	3.2	2.6	2.5	2.1	6.8	8.9	4.7	4.6	7.3	6.3
28.7	29.3	28.8	28.6	..	29.6	29.9	30.7	26.9	28.1	..	14.8
31.9	31.7	31.6	32.0	..	32.6	31.1	33.6	32.4	31.1	..	18.0
24.0	23.6	24.6	23.9	24.5	24.0	32.5	14.6	2.9	17.3	23.3	29.3
32.8	31.5	30.2	29.0	27.9	34.5	39.5	48.4	13.8	55.6	40.2	17.9
96.0	97.0	96.0	..	..	94.6	78.6	85.7	94.1	89.1	83.3	89.6
..	..	..	..	..	80.0	94.0	94.5	96.5	78.5	87.0	77.0
..	..	..	..	..	76.0	73.0	90.5	98.5	68.5	80.3	48.4
120.2	118.5	118.2	..	..	116.5	106.5	96.8	81.8	80.2	95.6	112.1
68.4	72.9	74.6	..	..	59.0	62.9	77.2	58.9	37.6	61.7	62.8
9.2	9.3	9.5	9.6	9.7	9.0	28.1	58.8	4.2	26.6	269.9	2043.0
1.4	1.3	1.3	1.1	1.2	1.6	1.9	2.0	3.8	1.8	2.1	1.1
63.4	64.1	64.8	65.5	66.1	62.2	54.6	43.1	76.9	52.3	55.6	42.0
71.9	72.1	72.1	72.1	..	71.3	69.4	65.2	70.2	65.6	66.0	68.5
2.4	2.2	2.1	2.1	..	2.6	3.8	3.6	4.4	3.4	4.0	2.3
27.6	26.6	26.2	25.8	..	30.7	38.6	52.7	27.8	56.8	51.7	37.9
123.8	121.8	121.2	..	..	121.0	112.9	102.9	81.2	91.2	102.3	113.9
116.5	115.0	115.0	..	..	111.8	99.8	90.4	82.4	68.7	88.6	110.3
21.9	20.8	19.7	18.6	17.7	23.3	29.1	36.2	6.9	42.1	28.8	11.1
43.8	42.3	40.9	39.4	38.1	45.9	50.0	60.9	21.4	68.9	52.0	24.8

Table A.2b	Poverty and Inequality in Tunisia, Egypt, Morocco, and Jordan						
	Urban		Rural		Overall		
Country and survey year	Headcount index (%)	Poverty gap (%)	Headcount index (%)	Poverty gap (%)	Headcount index (%)	Poverty gap (%)	Gini coefficient
Tunisia							
1985	4.6	NA	19.1	NA	11.2	NA	0.406
1990	3.5	0.7	13.1	3.2	7.4	1.7	NA
1995	3.6	0.7	13.9	3.1	7.6	1.6	0.400
2000	1.7		8.3		4.1		0.4
Egypt							
1981/82	18.2	3.5	16.1	3.1	17.2	NA	0.394
1990/91	20.3	4.3	28.6	4.5	25.0	NA	NA
1995/96	22.5	4.9	23.3	4.3	22.9	NA	0.320
1997	22.5	5.6	24.3	6.4	23.5	6.7	0.320
1999/00	3.7		18.3		16.7		
Morocco							
1984/85	17.3	NA	32.6	NA	26.0	NA	0.446
1990/91	7.6	1.5	18.0	3.8	13.1	2.7	NA
1998/99	12.0	2.5	27.2	6.7	19.0	4.4	0.395
Jordan							
1986/87	2.6	NA	4.4	NA	3.0	0.3	0.36
1992	12.4	3.1	21.1	5.1	14.4	3.6	0.40
1997	10.0	2.1	18.2	4.0	11.7	2.5	0.36
1999[a]					12.0	3.03	0.36
2001[a]					11.6	3.01	0.36

a. World Bank, 2002, p. 11.

Sources: Adams and Page 2003.

Table A.2c	Comparing National and International Poverty Lines for Selected Countries in the MNA Region				
Country	Survey year	National poverty lines Population below the poverty line (%)	Survey year	International poverty lines Population below $1.00/person/day (%)	Population below $2.00/person/day (%)
Algeria	1995	22.6	1995	< 2	15.1
Egypt	1997	23.5	1995	3.1	52.7
Jordan	1997	11.7	1997	< 2	7.4
Morocco	1998/99	19.0	1990/91	< 2	7.5
Tunisia	1995	7.6	1995	< 2	10.0
West Bank & Gaza	1998	23.2	NA	NA	NA
Yemen	1991/92	19.1	1998	15.7	45.2

Source: World Bank 2003b.

Table A.2d Social Indicators in Tunisia and Comparator Countries, 1975–80

Indicator	Tunisia				Algeria				
	1975	1978	1979	1980	1975	1978	1979	1980	1975
Life expectancy at birth, total (years)	58.6	..	..	62.4	56.3	..	..	59	53
Life expectancy at birth, female (years)	59.3	..	..	63.5	57.3	..	..	60	55
Life expectancy at birth, male (years)	57.8	..	..	61.4	55.3	..	..	58	52
Infant mortality rate (per 1,000 live births)	94.4	..	..	69.2	120	..	..	98	139
Birth rate, crude (per 1,000 people)	36.7	..	..	34.8	46.2	..	..	42	39
Death rate, crude (per 1,000 people)	10.9	..	..	9	14.2	..	..	12	15
Fertility rate, total (births per woman)	5.9	..	..	5.2	7.3	..	..	6.7	5.4
Improved water source (% of population with access)									
Improved water source, urban (% of urban population with access)	..	..	..	..	..	..	..	..	..
Improved water source, rural (% of rural population with access)	..	..	..	..	..	..	..	..	..
Immunization, DPT (% of children under 12 months)	..	..	..	36	..	..	..	..	..
Immunization, measles (% of children under 12 months)	..	..	..	65	..	..	..	..	..
Sanitation (% of population with access)	..	..	..	..	..	..	..	..	..
Illiteracy rate, adult total (% of people ages 15 and above)	63.8	58.6	56.8	55.1	69.2	65	63	61	65
Illiteracy rate, adult female (% of females ages 15 and above)	77.1	72.3	70.5	68.8	83.2	79	78	76	79
Illiteracy rate, adult male (% of males ages 15 and above)	50.6	45	43.3	41.7	53.9	49	47	46	50
Sanitation, rural (% of rural population with access)	..	..	..	..	..	..	..	..	..
Sanitation, urban (% of urban population with access)	..	..	..	..	..	..	..	..	..
School enrollment, primary (% net)	..	..	..	82.2	76.6	..	..	81	..
School enrollment, primary, female (% net)	..	..	..	71.8	63.9	..	..	71	..
School enrollment, primary, male (% net)	..	..	..	92.1	88.9	..	..	91	..
School enrollment, secondary (% net)	16.3	..	..	22.9	..	..	..	31	..
School enrollment, secondary, female (% net)	12.2	..	..	17.3	..	..	..	24	..
School enrollment, secondary, male (% net)	20.3	..	..	28.2	..	..	..	37	..
School enrollment, secondary (% gross)	21.1	..	..	27	20	..	..	33	40
Pupil-teacher ratio, primary	40	..	..	38.5	40.9	..	..	35	35
Land use, arable land (% of land area)	22.1	22	21.9	20.5	2.9	2.9	2.9	2.9	2.7
Labor force, total (millions)	1.8	2.0	2.1	2.2	4.1	4.5	4.7	4.9	12.7
Labor force, female (% of total labor force)	26.3	27.9	28.4	28.9	20.9	21.2	21.3	21.4	26.2

Source: World Bank, *World Development Indicators* (various issues).

Egypt			Morocco				Jordan				MNA			
1978	1979	1980	1975	1978	1979	1980	1975	1978	1979	1980	1975	1978	1979	1980
..	..	56	55	..	..	58	..	..	..	..	46	..	..	47.6
..	..	57	56	..	..	59.8	..	..	..	..	47.8	..	..	49.4
..	..	54	53	..	..	56.3	..	..	..	..	44.4	..	..	46
..	..	120	115	..	..	99.2	48.8	..	..	40.8	125	..	..	115
..	..	39	42	..	..	38.1	..	..	..	..	47.6	0	0	46.8
..	..	13	14	..	..	12	..	..	..	..	18.9	0	0	17.5
..	..	5.1	6.3	..	..	5.4	7.5	..	..	6.8	6.6	..	..	6.6
..	..	..	..	..	..	..	..	..	..	...	..	..	..	..
..	..	..	..	..	..	..	..	..	..	..	..	..	..	..
..	..	..	..	..	..	..	..	..	..	..	..	..	..	..
..	82	84	..	..	..	..	..	..	..	30	..	..	..	..
..	62	78	..	..	..	..	..	..	..	29	..	..	..	..
..	..	..	..	..	..	..	..	..	..	..	..	..	..	..
62	62	61	76	73	72	71.5	38.6	35.7	56.8	31.6	66.9	63.8	62.8	61.7
77	76	75	88	86	85	84.6	56.2	51.9	70.5	46.1	77.3	74.4	73.3	72.2
48	47	47	62	60	59	58	22.1	20.3	43.3	17.9	56.1	52.8	51.7	50.6
..	..	..	..	..	..	..	..	..	..	..	..	..	..	..
..	..	..	..	..	..	..	..	..	..	..	..	..	..	..
..	..	..	47	..	..	61.6	78.6	..	..	73	..	..	..	..
..	..	..	35	..	..	47.4	73.4	..	..	72.6	..	..	..	..
..	..	..	58	..	..	75.1	83.6	..	..	73.4	..	..	..	..
..	..	..	14	..	..	20.3	44.2	..	..	52.8	..	..	..	..
..	..	..	10	..	..	15.7	37.2	..	..	50.8	..	..	..	..
..	..	..	17	..	..	24.8	50.9	..	..	54.6	..	..	..	..
..	..	51	17	..	..	26	47.5	..	..	59.1	9.9	..	..	15
..	..	..	42	..	..	38.2	34.7	..	..	31.8	..	..	..	..
2.4	2.3	2.3	16	17	17	16.9	3.3	3.3	21.9	3.4	5.3	5.4	5.4	5.5
13.6	13.9	14.3	6.0	6.6	6.8	7.0	0.5	0.5	0.5	0.5	149.5	161.4	165.7	170.3
26.4	26.4	26.5	32.5	33.1	33.3	33.5	14.1	14.5	14.6	14.7	23.2	23.6	23.7	23.8

| Table A.2e | Social Indicators for Tunisia and Comparator Countries, 1996–01 |

Indicator	Tunisia						Algeria						
	1996	1997	1998	1999	2000	2001	1996	1997	1998	1999	2000	2001	1996
Life expectancy at birth, total (years)	..	72	72	72	..	72	..	70	..	71	..		..
Life expectancy at birth, female (years)	..	74	74	74	..		..	72	..	73	..		..
Life expectancy at birth, male (years)	..	70	71	71	..		..	69	..	69	..		..
Infant mortality rate (per 1,000 live births)	30	28	25	24	..		37	35	..	34	..		..
Birth rate, crude (per 1,000 people)	20	19	18	17	..		..	27	..	25	..		..
Death rate, crude (per 1,000 people)	5.5	5.6	5.6	5.6	..		6	6.1	..	5.6	..		..
Fertility rate, total (births per woman)	2.5	2.4	2.2	2.2	..		..	3.6	..	3.4	..		..
Improved water source (% of population with access)	..	..	..	..	..		..	..	..	..	94		..
Improved water source, urban (% of urban population with access)	..	..	..	..	..		..	..	..	..	98		..
Improved water source, rural (% of rural population with access)	..	..	..	..	..		..	..	..	..	88		..
Immunization, DPT (% of children under 12 months)	91	96	96	100	..		77	79	80	83	..		91
Immunization, measles (% of children under 12 months)	86	92	94	93	..		75	74	75	78	..		92
Sanitation (% of population with access)	..	..	..	..	..		..	..	..	..	73		..
Illiteracy rate, adult total (% of people ages 15 and above)	34	33	31	30	29	28	37	36	35	33	32	32	48
Illiteracy rate, adult female (% of females ages 15 and above)	45	44	42	41	39		49	47	46	44	43		60
Illiteracy rate, adult male (% of males ages 15 and above)	23	22	21	20	19	18	26	25	24	23	22	23	36
Sanitation, rural (% of rural population with access)	..	..	..	..	..		..	..	..	..	47		..
Sanitation, urban (% of urban population with access)	..	..	..	..	..		..	..	..	..	90		..
School enrollment, primary (% net)	98	..	98	..	..		94	..	94	..	..		93
School enrollment, primary, female (% net)	96	..	96	..	..		91	..	92	..	..		88
School enrollment, primary, male (% net)	99	..	99	..	..		97	..	96	..	..		98
School enrollment, secondary (% net)	..	..	..	..	..		56	..	58	..	..		68
School enrollment, secondary, female (% net)	..	..	..	..	..		55	..	59	..	..		64
School enrollment, secondary, male (% net)	..	..	..	..	..		58	..	58	..	..		71
School enrollment, secondary (% gross)	65	64	73	..	..		63	..	66	..	..		75
Pupil-teacher ratio, primary	25	24	25	..	..		27	27	..	..	..		27
Land use, arable land (% of land area)	19	19	19	..	..		3.2	3.2	3.2	..	..		2.8
Labor force, total (millions)	3.4	3.5	3.6	3.7	3.8	3.9	9	9.3	9.6	9.9	10	11	22
Labor force, female (% of total labor force)	30.7	30.9	31.2	31.4	31.7	31.9	25.1	25.7	26.4	27.0	27.6	28.3	29.0

Source: World Bank, *World Development Indicators* (various issues).

Egypt					Jordan						Morocco						MNA					
1997	1998	1999	2000	2001	1996	1997	1998	1999	2000	2001	1996	1997	1998	1999	2000	2001	1996	1997	1998	1999	2000	2001
66	..	67	..		..	71	..	71	..		..	67	..	67	..		..	49	..	68	..	
68	..	68	..		..	73	..	73	..		..	69	..	69	..		..	50	..	48	..	
65	..	65	..		..	69	..	70	..		..	65	..	65	..		..	47	..	46	..	
51	..	47	..		..	28	..	26	..		..	51	..	48	..		..	93	..	43	..	
26	..	26	..		..	31	..	30	..		..	26	..	25	..		0	41	0.1	40	..	
7	..	6.9	..		..	4.4	..	4.2	..		..	6.8	..	6.6	..		0	16	0	16	..	
3.4	..	3.3	..		..	3.9	3.8	3.7	..		3.3	3.1	..	2.9	..		..	5.5	..	3	..	
..	..	..	95		..	..	..	..	96		..	..	..	..	82		..	..	..	..	89	
..	..	..	96		..	..	..	..	100		..	..	..	..	100		..	..	..	..	82	
..	..	..	94		..	..	..	..	84		..	..	..	..	58		..	..	..	..	41	
94	96	95	..		100	93	91	85	..		95	95	93	94	..		53	53	48	59	..	
92	98	96	..		98	95	86	83	..		93	92	91	93	..		54	58	50	57	..	
..	..	..	94		..	..	..	..	99		..	..	..	..	75		..	..	..	..	55	
47	46	45	45	44	13	12	11	11	10	9.8	55	54	53	52	51	50	43	42	41	39	38	34
59	58	57	56		19	18	17	17	16		68	67	66	65	64		52	50	49	47	46	
35	35	34	33	33	6.6	6.2	5.8	5.5	5.2	4.6	41	41	40	39	38	37	34	33	32	31	30	24
..	..	..	91		..	..	..	..	98		..	..	..	..	42		..	..	..	..	41	
..	..	..	98		..	..	..	..	100		..	..	..	..	100		..	..	..	..	81	
..	92	..	..		..	..	83	..	..		74	..	79	..	..		..	..	..	..	..	
..	89	..	..		..	..	83	..	..		65	..	..	..	..		..	..	..	..	..	
..	95	..	..		..	..	82	..	..		83	..	85	..	..		..	..	..	..	..	
..	..	..	..		..	..	72	..	..		..	..	..	..	..		..	..	..	..	..	
..	..	..	..		..	..	75	..	..		..	..	..	..	..		..	..	..	..	..	
..	..	..	..		..	..	70	..	..		..	..	..	..	..		..	..	..	..	..	
78	81	..	..		56	57	80	..	..		39	..	40	..	..		..	..	..	..	..	
23	24	..	..		21	21	25	..	..		28	28	28	..	..		..	..	..	..	..	
2.8	2.8	..	..		2.8	2.9	2.9	..	..		20	20	20	..	..		6.5	6.5	6.5	..	..	
22	23	24	24	25	1.2	1.3	1.3	1.4	1.5	1.5	10	11	11	11	12	12	260	268	275	282	289	290
29.4	29.7	30.1	30.4	30.7	22	23	23	24	25	25	34.6	34.6	34.7	34.7	34.7	34.8	26.2	26.6	26.9	27.3	27.7	28.1

Table A.2f	Tunisia: Privatization and Restructuring by Sector (1987 to August 2003)			
	Volume		Number of enterprises	
Sector	Million TD	%	Number	%
Agriculture, fisheries, and agro-industry	**72.0**	**3.2**	**18.0**	**10.7**
Industry	**952.0**	**40.6**	**56.0**	**33.3**
Construction materials	825.0	35.1	18.0	10.7
Mechanical, electrical, and chemical industries	108.0	4.6	30.0	17.9
Textiles	19.0	0.8	8.0	4.8
Services	**1,318.0**	**56.2**	**94.0**	**56.0**
Tourism and handicrafts	277.0	11.8	37.0	22.0
Commerce	137.0	5.8	21.0	12.5
Transport	69.0	3.0	16.0	9.5
Others	835.0	35.6	20.0	11.9
Total	**2,346.0**	**100.0**	**168.0**	**100.0**

Source: Directorate of Privatization, Government of Tunisia.

Table A.2g	Tunisia: Foreign Investment in Privatization (1987 to August 31, 2003)	
Sector	Receipts from foreign investors	Percentage of total
Agriculture, fishing, and food	**0**	**0**
Industries	**782**	**44.6**
Construction materials	771	43.9
Chemical and mechanical industries	6	0.3
Textiles	5	0.3
Services	**974**	**55.5**
Tourism and handicrafts	93	5.3
Transport	17	1.0
Trade	76	4.3
Others	788	44.9
Total	**1,755**	**100.0**

Source: Ministry of Economic Development, Government of Tunisia.

Table A.2h	Tunisia: Privatization and Restructuring by Sector (October 1998 to August 2003)	
Sector	**Receipts, million TD**	**Percentage of total**
Agriculture, fishing, and food	**24**	**1**
Industries	**855**	**45**
Construction materials	798	42
Chemical and mechanical industries	51	3
Textiles	6	0
Services	**205**	**11**
Tourism and handicrafts	143	8
Transport	0	0
Trade	62	3
Others	**806**	**43**
Total	**1,891**	**100**

Source: Ministry of Economic Development, Government of Tunisia.

Table A.2i	Tunisia: Privatization Types (between 1982 and August 31, 2003)	
Type	**Number of enterprises**	**Percentage of total**
Full privatization	87	52
Partial privatization	31	18
Liquidation	38	23
Others	10	6
Concession	2	1
Total	**168**	**100**

Note: Total receipts amounted to 2,346 MDT.

Source: Privatization Directorate, Government of Tunisia.

Table A.2j	Tunisia: Mode of Privatization (between 1982 and August 31, 2003)	
Mode	**Privatization proceeds in MDT**	**Percentage of total**
Sales of shares	1,239	53
Sales of asset/capital (Vente d'éléments d'actif)	352	15
Concession	756	32
Total	**2,346**	**100**

Source: Privatization Directorate, Government of Tunisia.

Table A.2k	Trade and Openness: Tunisia and Comparator Countries	
Country/Region	**1985**	**2000**
Algeria	50	64
Egypt, Arab Rep. of	52	39
Jordan	113	110
Morocco	60	69
Tunisia	70	92
MNA	**45**	**59**

Source: Adams and Page 2003b; World Bank, *World Development Indicators*.

Table A.2l	Average Tariff Rates in Selected Countries (weighted, %)	
Country	**1992–95**	**2001–02**
Algeria	16.1	7.6
Egypt, Arab Rep. of	17.1	9.7
Jordan	n.a.	11.1
Morocco	47.0	27.9
Tunisia	30.0	27.4
Chile	10.98	7
Korea, Rep. of	6.94	5.68
Mauritius	22.64	15.76
Malaysia	4.7	5.17
Thailand	13.18	9.33

Source: World Bank, World Integrated Trade Solutions (WITS) as of October 2003.

Table A.2m	Tunisia: Summary Tariff Statistics, 2000–02					
	MFN tariffs			**EU-preferential tariffs**		
	2000	**2001**	**2002**	**2000**	**2001**	**2002**
Average	35.9	35.9	34.5	28.5	25.6	24.3
Agricultural	77.1	77.1	71.6	77.2	76.7	76.6
Nonagricultural	25	25	22.8	16	12.5	10.9
Maximum	220	220	215	n.a.	n.a.	n.a.

Source: IMF 2003, table 2, p. 20.

Table A.2n	Tunisia: Investment, Competition, and Banking Laws

A new unified Investment Code, adopted in December 1993 under EFRSL, represented an important improvement over the previous system.

A revised Banking Law and a new regulatory framework for mutual funds were submitted to the Chamber of Deputies in the context of ECAL II.

Overall, the law complied with international standards and represented good progress in ensuring an adequate legal framework for the sector.

An amended Civil and Commercial Procedures Code in 2003 to facilitate the judicial process for recovering loans under ECAL II.

A law prohibiting noncompetitive pricing was passed under EFRSL in the early 1990.

Table A.2o	Categories of Investment in Five Most Recently Closed Education Projects and in the Ongoing Quality Project (EQIP)

	Project/actual costs ($ million except for EQIP)					
Category	EQIP 1 (2000–05)	Sec. ed. support (1995–02)	Higher ed. restructuring (1992–02)	Employment & training fund (1990–97)	Education & training sector loan (1989–97)	Fifth ed. project (1983–90)
School infrastructure	122	150	59	-	114	8.7
Equipment/information and communications technology	49	-	-	-	54.7	18
Training/technical assistance/ innovation	11	7.3	15	18.5	2.8	0.5
Management/administration/ systemic improvements	0.3	-	3	2.2	-	-
Total	182	157.3	77	20.7	172	27

Note: Costs are projected costs for the EQIP project and actual for the other project.

Source: Internal World Bank data.

ANNEX A.3: EXTERNAL ASSISTANCE TO TUNISIA

Table A.3a	Tunisia: Net Receipts of External Financial Resources (US$million)											
	1990	**1991**	**1992**	**1993**	**1994**	**1995**	**1996**	**1997**	**1998**	**1999**	**2000**	**2001**
All donors	619.9	333.5	696.5	717.9	694.5	1,510.9	650.7	522.6	499.3	622.1	665.5	729.6
World Bank	103.2	172.8	−35.4	108.6	14.6	−68.4	−3.1	−48.9	−39.3	41.0	−16.9	144.7
IBRD	102.0	172.0	−36.9	101.2	15.3	−64.7	14.6	−45.8	−36.5	43.8	−14.5	146.9
IDA	−1.0	−2.0	−1.9	−2.0	−2.1	−2.1	−2.1	−2.1	−2.1	−2.1	−2.1	−2.1
IFC	2.2	2.8	3.4	9.4	1.4	−1.6	−15.6	−0.9	−0.6	−0.6	−0.3	−
World Food Program	13.6	3.4	2.6	3.7	3.7	3.9	2.5	4.0	−0.1	−	−	−
France	11.0	−101.8	142.6	105.9	105.3	118.8	103.9	65.3	192.1	257.2	35.7	139.5
Germany	23.4	21.6	52.7	50.2	22.8	−16.0	3.5	180.3	−15.0	−69.2	28.9	24.2
Japan	14.8	−263.1	−70.8	10.2	380.2	530.9	284.4	14.8	15.1	45.8	119.5	117.8
Sweden	28.4	32.9	12.6	20.7	9.7	0.2	−7.3	−6.4	0.7	−0.9	4.4	1.5
United Kingdom	15.0	13.8	103.4	1.2	8.4	−1.4	4.3	4.1	43.9	−3.3	50.8	−26.8
United States	24.0	8.0	−1.0	−14.0	−13.0	766.0	2.0	51.0	−5.4	−48.0	4.0	−30.0
Arab countries	105.0	−3.0	−4.4	−4.5	−15.1	−22.6	−38.3	−20.5	−32.0	−18.4	−11.5	−1.5
Arab agencies	32.0	28.5	46.8	34.1	3.0	−0.8	0.7	0.1	0.5	0.4	−0.4	−1.1
EC/EU	205.4	166.3	582.8	393.1	171.0	164.0	307.8	467.0	424.0	329.6	619.1	333.0
Others	44.4	254.1	−135.4	8.8	4.1	36.4	−9.7	−188.2	−85.2	88.0	−168.1	28.4
Net receipts												
Algeria	641	1,968	−1,062	−15	661	548	1876	−391	203	−934	−384	552
Egypt, Rep. of	3,311	4,237	1,661	2,677	3,228	2,441	2,737	2,916	4,119	1,771	3,242	2,800
Jordan	1,087	747	404	118	465	944	846	503	611	511	573	490
Morocco	1,620	1,888	1,182	746	811	617	812	549	895	587	586	377

Source: OECD 2003.

Table A.3b	Tunisia: World Bank Flows, 1990–03 (US$million)													
	1990	**1991**	**1992**	**1993**	**1994**	**1995**	**1996**	**1997**	**1998**	**1999**	**2000**	**2001**	**2002**	**2003**
Commitments	147	68	385	144	268	273	99	242	222	194	202	76	253	112
Net disbursements	140	109	58	27	14	10	−57	28	−48	33	−16	28	77	−19
Net transfers	47	−1	−56	−92	−106	−118	−182	−80	−145	−62	−99	−48	−3	−79
Net disbursements per capita (US$)	*17.2*	*13.1*	*6.8*	*3.1*	*1.6*	*1.1*	*−6.3*	*3.0*	*−5.2*	*3.5*	*−1.7*	*2.9*	*7.9*	*−1.9*

Table A.3c	Algeria: World Bank Flows, 1990–03 (US$ million)													
	1990	1991	1992	1993	1994	1995	1996	1997	1998	1999	2000	2001	2002	2003
Commitments	458	431	215	240	140	331	428	89	150	0	98	42	31	89
Net disbursements	171	95	236	36	9	203	256	−131	−4	−147	−119	−105	−104	−114
Net transfers	95	11	127	−80	−104	77	112	−260	−118	−276	−248	−229	−217	−188
Net disbursements per capita (US$)[a]	6.8	3.7	9.0	1.3	0.3	7.2	9.0	−4.5	−0.1	−4.9	−3.9	−3.4	−3.3	−3.6

Table A.3d	Egypt: World Bank Flows, 1990–03 (US$ million)													
	1990	1991	1992	1993	1994	1995	1996	1997	1998	1999	2000	2001	2002	2003
Commitments	62	524	376	338	121	80	172	75	142	550	50	0	50	12
Net disbursements	−70	−98	−60	33	−16	−84	−67	−55	29	−51	−38	−57	−48	−26
Net transfers	−207	−249	−184	−92	−136	−207	−180	−146	−41	−114	−94	−105	−87	−53
Net disbursements per capita (US$)	−1.3	−1.8	−1.1	0.6	−0.3	−1.5	−1.1	−0.9	0.5	−0.8	−0.6	−0.9	−0.7	−0.4

Table A.3e	Morocco: World Bank Flows, 1990–03 (US$ million)													
	1990	1991	1992	1993	1994	1995	1996	1997	1998	1999	2000	2001	2002	2003
Commitments	483	626	325	549	412	58	540	108	200	440	8	98	5	4
Net disbursements	189	135	263	58	19	−102	141	−24	−31	113	−227	−130	−218	−197
Net transfers	−20	−103	22	−201	−245	−381	−134	−274	−249	−103	−427	−310	−375	−305
Net disbursements per capita (US$)	7.9	5.5	10.5	2.3	0.7	−3.9	5.3	−0.9	−1.1	4.0	−7.9	−4.5	−7.3	−6.5

Table A.3f	Jordan: World Bank Flows, 1990–03 (US$ million)													
	1990	1991	1992	1993	1994	1995	1996	1997	1998	1999	2000	2001	2002	2003
Commitments	175	25	0	55	100	147	120	140	67	210	35	120	5	120
Net disbursements	78	−17	21	38	22	31	40	109	−7	89	−24	103	−10	99
Net transfers	43	−61	−20	−4	−22	−17	−9	63	−56	41	−75	50	−53	70
Net disbursements per capita (US$)	24.7	−4.7	5.5	9.8	5.4	7.3	9.2	24.5	−1.5	18.7	−4.9	20.6	−1.9	18.5

Note: Until April 29, 2003.

a. 2002 and 2003 population figures extrapolated using 2001 population growth rate.

Source: World Bank data as of April 29, 2003.

Annex A.4	Selected ESW and CAS List for Tunisia			
Report title	**Report type***	**Date**	**Report #**	**Year**
1. Tunisia – Country Assistance Strategy	CAS	03/28/00	20161	2000
Agriculture				
1. From Universal Food Subsidies to a Self-Targeted Program: A Case Study in Tunisian Reform	Pub	12/31/96	WDP351	1996
Economic Policy				
1. Morocco, Tunisia – Export Growth: Determinants and Prospects	SR	10/31/94	12947	1994
2. Tunisia – Poverty Alleviation: Preserving Progress while Preparing for the Future (Vol. 1-2)	SR	08/31/95	13993	1995
3. Tunisia – Towards the 21st Century (Vol. 1-2)	ER	10/31/95	14375	1995
4. Logistical Constraints on International Trade in the Maghreb	PRWP	05/31/96	WPS1598	1996
5. From Universal Food Subsidies to a Self-Targeted Program	SR	06/30/96	15878	1996
6. Tunisia's Global Integration and Sustainable Development: Strategic Choices for 21st Century	Pub	08/31/96	15966	1996
7. Implementation of Uruguay Round Commitments: The Development Challenges	PRWP	10/31/99	WPS2215	1999
8. Trade Policy Developments in the Middle East and North Africa	Pub	02/29/00	20322	2000
9. Exports and Information Spillovers	PRWP	11/30/00	WPS2474	2000
Education				
1. Tunisia – Higher Education: Challenges and Opportunities	SR	05/08/97	16522	1997
2. Education in the Middle East and North Africa: A Strategy towards Learning for Development	WP	04/30/99	21589	1999
3. L'Enseignement Superieur Tunisien: Enjeux et Avenir	Pub	03/31/98	17493	1998
Energy				
1. Tunisia – Inter-fuel Substitution Study: A Joint Report	ESMAP	05/31/90	ESM114	1990
2. Tunisia – Power Efficiency Study	ESMAP	02/29/92	ESM136	1992
3. Tunisia – Energy Management Strategy in Residential and Tertiary Sectors	ESMAP	04/30/92	ESM146	1992
4. Increasing the Efficiency of Gas Distribution – Phase 1: Case Studies and Thematic Data Sheets	ESMAP	07/31/99	ESM218	1999
Environment				
1. The Greening of the Economic Policy Reform (Vol. 1-2)	EWP	02/28/97	16339	1997
Finance				
1. External Finance in the Middle East – Trends and Prospects	DWP	12/31/93	20956	1993
2. Making Micro Finance Work in the Middle East and North Africa	WP	12/31/98	23076	1998
Health				
1. How Access to Contraception Affects Fertility and Contraceptive Use in Tunisia	PRWP	01/31/92	WPS841	1992
2. Towards a Virtuous Circle: Nutrition Review of MNA	DWP	08/31/99	20960	1999
3. Risks and Macroeconomic Impact of HIV/AIDS in the Middle East and North Africa: Why Waiting to Intervene Can Be Costly	PRWP	08/31/02	WPS2874	2002

Report title	Report type*	Date	Report #	Year
Multisector				
1. The World Bank Research Observer	Pub	02/28/98	17258	1998
Others				
1. Strengthening Tunisian Municipalities to Foster Local Urban Development	OEDRP	01/01/01	24568	2001
3. The World Bank in Action: Stories of Development	WP	01/01/02	24928	2002
3. Initiative in Legal and Judicial Reform	WP	03/31/02	25082	2002
Social Protection and Poverty Analysis				
1. Options for Pension Reforms in Tunisia	PRWP	07/31/93	WPS1154	1993
2. Tunisia's Insurance Sector	PRWP	05/31/95	WPS1451	1995
3. Tunisia – Social Structure Review 2000: Integrating into the World Economy and Sustaining Economic and Social Progress	WP	06/30/00	20976	2000
Private Sector Development				
1. Privatization in Tunisia	DWP	01/31/93	11645	1993
2. Tunisia – Private Sector Assessment	SR	11/30/94	12945	1994
3. Tunisia – Private Sector Assessment Update - Meeting the Challenge of Globalization (Vol.1-3)	SR	12/14/00	20173	2000
4. Is Inequality Bad for Business: A Non-Linear Microeconomic Model of Wealth Effects on Self-Employment	PRWP	01/31/01	WPS2527	2001
Public Sector Management				
1. Partners for Development: New Roles for Government and the Private Sector in the Middle East and North Africa	Pub	09/30/99	19807	1999
Transportation				
1. Optimal User Charges and Cost Recovery for Roads in Developing Countries	PRWP	10/31/91	WPS780	1991
Urban Development				
1. The Urban Age – Innovations in Urban Management 3 (4)	Newsletter	01/31/96	17449	1996
Water Supply and Sanitation				
1. Water Pricing Experiences: An International Perspective	Pub	10/31/97	WTP386	1997

Abbreviations:

CAS: Country Assistance Strategy

DWP: Departmental Working Paper

ER : Economic Report

ESMAP: Working Paper, Economic & Social Council for Asia & Pacific

EWP: Environmental Working Paper

OEDAR: OED Annual Report/Review

PRWP: Policy Research Working Paper

Pub: Publication

SR: Sector Report

Source: Imagebank, Word Bank. These documents can be accessed at World Development Sources at www-wds.worldbank.org.

ANNEX A.5: EVALUATION RATINGS

Table A.5a	Ratings for Tunisia and Comparator Countries							
		o/w:	Outcome (%)		Sustainability (%)[a]		Inst. development impact (%)[a]	
Country	Total evaluated	Adjustment ($m)	Satisf	Satisf. adj.	Likely	Likely adj.	Substan.	Sub-stan. adj
Before 1990								
Tunisia	**2,180**	**533**	**91**	**100**	**73**	**72**	**20**	**29**
MNA	14,282	1,897	76	87	48	45	30	59
Algeria	2,056	..	48	..	7	..	1	..
Egypt, Rep. of	3,130	70	83	0	56	0	19	0
Jordan	753	..	77	0	51	..	31	..
Morocco	4,177	1,256	81	88	52	38	51	76
Bankwide	186,355	29,568	71	68	53	55	33	34

a. The institutional development impact and sustainability ratings have been in use only since FY98. Hence, the data for these two ratings for the period before FY91 apply for smaller levels of total net commitment than shown in columns 2 and 3 of the table.

Source: OED internal database as of May 1, 2003.

	OED Evaluation Findings of Evaluated Projects (Exits FY90–03)							
	Net commit-ment (US$M)	O/w Adjustment (US$M)	Satisfactory outcome (%)		Likely sustainability (%)		Substantial ID (%)	
Country			Net commit-ment	O/w Adjust-ment	Net commit-ment	O/w Adjust-ment	Net commit-ment	O/w Adjust-ment
Tunisia	**2,367**	**967**	**81.8**	**86.5**	**83.8**	**100**	**41**	**17**
MNA	15,974	5,276	71.1	72.1	52.1	56.5	35	41
Algeria	3,253	1,099	45.8	41	7.2	0	21	27
Egypt, Rep. of	2,025	150	83.2	100	39.5	0	34	100
Jordan	1,534	870	93.6	100	79.5	90.8	49	63
Morocco	4,736	1984	67.2	67.6	38	46	58.9	51.4
Bankwide	251,234	87,978	75.9	76.9	65.5	71.9	43	44

Note: Sustainability and institutional development impact ratings have been in use only since FY98.

Source: OED internal data.

Table A.5b	Ratings for the Active Portfolio for Tunisia and Comparator Countries			
Country	**No. of projects**	**Net commit. ($m)**	**Projects at risk (%)**	**Commitments at risk (%)**
Tunisia	**18**	**1,168**	**11**	**6**
MNA	110	4,801	25	28
Algeria	13	566	38	52
Egypt, Rep. of	16	905	25	40
Jordan	6	192	17	18
Morocco	15	418	13	25
Bankwide	1,376	95,489	18	18

Source: World Bank data as of May 2003.

Table A.5c	All Approved Tunisia Projects, Evaluated and Ongoing, as of December 18, 2002			
Approval FY	**Exit FY**	**Project ID**	**Project name**	**Lending instrument type**
Agriculture				
1967	1974	P005595	Cooperative farm project	Investment
1972	1977	P005607	Agricultural credit project	Investment
1972	1980	P005608	Fisheries project	Investment
1975	1983	P005616	Irrigation rehabilitation project	Investment
1977	1982	P005622	Second agricultural credit project	Investment
1977	1984	P005623	Sidi Salem multipurpose project	Investment
1979	1987	P005629	Second fisheries project	Investment
1980	1987	P005633	Third agricultural credit project	Investment
1980	1987	P005633	Southern irrigation project	Investment
1997	2004	P005736	TN- Natural Resource Management	Investment
2000	2006	P035707	TN- Water Sector Investment Project	Investment
2001	2007	P005750	TN- Agriculture Support Services	Investment
Economic Policy				
1987	FY90	P005688	Industry & Trade Policy Adj.	Adjustment
1988	FY91	P005718	SAL I	Adjustment
1992	FY95	P005742	Econ. & Fin. Reform SU	Adjustment
Education				
1967	1976	P005596	Second education project	Investment
1976	1983	P005620	Third education project	Investment
1981	1989	P005640	Fourth education project	Investment
1983	FY90	P005650	Education V	Investment
1989	FY97	P005715	Edu. & Training Sector	Investment
1992	FY02	P005726	Higher Education Restructuring	Investment
1995	FY02	P005743	Secondary Education	Investment
1998	12/31/2003	P005741	TN-Higher Education Reform Support I	Investment
2000	6/30/2005	P050945	TN- Education PAQSET 1	Investment
Electric Power & Other Energy				
1972	1977	P005610	Power project	Investment
1977	1981	P005625	Second power project	Investment
1981	1986	P005643	Third power project	Investment
Energy and Mining				
1984	FY91	P005656	Mining Technical Assistance	Investment
1984	FY91	P005657	Power IV	Investment
1985	FY93	P005662	Elec. & Mec. Ind. II	Investment
1987	FY94	P005701	Energy Conservation Demonstr	Investment
1988	FY95	P005667	SMI - II	Investment
1989	FY94	P005729	Petroleum Explor. Pr.	Investment
1992	FY97	P005735	Gas Infrastructure	Investment

Commitment ($m)	Outcome	ID	Sustainability	APPI	Eval type	Latest DO	Latest IP	Latest risk rating
18	Unsat	NR	NR		PAR			
8	Sat	NR	NR		PAR			
2	Sat	NR	NR		PAR			
12.2	Sat	NR	NR		PCR			
12	Sat	NR	NR		PAR			
42	Sat	NR	NR		PAR			
28.5	Sat	Sub	Likely		PCR			
30	Sat	Modest	Likely		PAR			
25	Sat	NR	NR		PCR			
26.5						Sat	Sat	Modest
103.3						Sat	Sat	Modest
21.3						Sat	Sat	Sub
150	Sat	Modest	Likely	7.25	PAR			
150	Sat	Sub	Likely	8.25	PAR			
250	Sat	Modest	Likely	7.25	PAR	Sat	Sat	Sub
13	Sat	NR	NR		PAR			
8.9	Sat	NR	NR		PAR			
26	Sat	Modest	Likely		PAR			
27	Unsat	Neg	Uncertain	4	PCR			
95	Sat	Modest	Likely	7.25	PAR			
68.7	Sat	Subs	Likely	8.25	ES	Sat	Sat	Modest
91.3	Sat	Sub	Likely	8.25	ES	Sat	Sat	Neg
80.0						Sat	Sat	Modest
99.0						Sat	Sat	Sub
12	Sat	NR	NR		PAR			
14.5	Sat	NR	NR		PCR			
41.5	Sat	NR	NR		PCR			
13.4	Sat	Sub	Likely	8.25	PCR			
38.7	Mod. Sat	Neg	Likely	6	PCR			
54	Unsat	Modest	Unlikely	4.25	PAR			
4	Unsat	Modest	Likely	5	PAR			
28	Unsat	Neg	Unlikely	3.75	EVM			
5.5	Sat	Modest	Uncertain	6.75	EVM			
60	Sat	Modest	Likely	7.25	ES	Sat	Sat	Modest

(Table continues on the following page.)

Table A.5c		All Approved Tunisia Projects, Evaluated and Ongoing, as of December 18, 2002 (continue	
Approval FY	**Exit FY**	**Project ID**	**Project name**	**Lending instrument type**

Approval FY	Exit FY	Project ID	Project name	Lending instrument type
Environment				
1994	FY00	P005588	Mediterranean Pollution Control	Investment
1994	FY01	P005733	Mountainous Areas Dev.	Investment
1994	2003	P005591	Ozone Depleting Subs	Investment
2003	2003	P072317	TN- NW Mountainous & Forest Areas Dev.	Investment
Finance				
1968	1972	P005597	Second Societe Nationale d'Investissement project	Investment
1970	1975	P005602	Third Societe Nationale d'Investissement project	Investment
1972	1978	P005609	Fourth Societe Nationale d'Investissement project	Investment
1973	1978	P005612	Fifth Societe Nationale d'Investissement project	Investment
1976	1981	P005619	Sixth Societe Nationale d'Investissement project	Investment
1978	1983	P005627	Industrial finance project - BDET component	Investment
2002	6/30/2003	P055815	TN- ECAL III	Adjustment
Financial Sector				
1985	FY92	P005663	Export Industries	Investment
1994	FY01	P005748	Private Investment Credit	Investment
1997	FY98	P042287	ECAL I	Adjustment
1999	FY01	P053255	TN- ECAL II	Adjustment
Health, Nutrition & Population				
1991	FY98	P005717	Population and Family	Investment
1991	FY00	P005738	Hospital Mgmt. & Fin.	Investment
1971	1979	P005604	Population Project	Investment
1981	1989	P005642	Health and Population	Investment
1998	12/31/2003	P005746	TN- Health Sector Loan	Investment
Industry				
1981	1989	P005639	Small-scale industry development	Investment
1981	1984	P005641	SOGITEX textile rehabilitation project	Investment
1996	12/31/2003	P040208	TN- Industry Support Institution	Investment
Mining				
1975	1979	P005617	Phosphate project	Investment
Oil & Gas				
1971	1974	P005606	El Borma - Gades gas pipeline project	Investment
1980	1974	P005635	Second natural gas pipeline project	Investment
1995	6/30/2004	P005589	Solar Water Heating	Investment
Public Sector Governance				
1990	FY93	P005710	Public Enterprise I	Adjustment
Rural Sector				
1981	FY90	P005638	Northwest Reg. Proj.	Investment
1983	FY91	P005649	Central Tunisia Irrigation	Investment

Commitment ($m)	Outcome	ID	Sustainability	APPI	Eval type	Latest DO	Latest IP	Latest risk rating
0	Sat	Sub	Likely	8.25	ES	H Sat.	H Sat.	Neg
26.4	Mod Sat	Subs	Likely	7.5	ES	Sat	Sat	Modest
3.8						Sat	Sat	Low or
								Neg.
34						Sat	Sat	Sub
10	Sat	NR	NR		PAR			
10	Sat	NR	NR		PAR			
10	Sat	NR	NR		PAR			
14	Sat	NR	NR		PAR			
20	Sat	NR	NR		PAR			
30	Sat	NR	NR		PAR			
252.5						Sat	Sat	Sub
50	Mod. Sat	Modest	Likely	5.75	PAR			
118.8	Sat	Sub	Likely	8.25	ES	Sat	Sat	Neg
69.9	Sat	NR	Likely		ES	Sat	Sat	Modest
134	Sat	Modest	Likely	7.25	ES	Sat	Sat	Neg
26	Highly Sat	Sub	Likely	10	ES	H Sat.	H. Sat	Neg
29.7	Sat	Sub	Likely	8.25	ES			
9.6	Unsat	NR	NR		PAR			
12.5	Sat	Sub	Likely		PAR			
50.0						Sat	Sat	Modest
30	Sat	Modest	Likely		PCR			
18.6	Sat	NR	NR		PAR			
38.7						Sat	Sat	Modest
23.3	Sat	NR	NR		PCR			
7.5	Sat	NR	NR		PAR			
37	Sat	Modest	Likely		PAR			
7.4						Sat	Sat	Modest
130	Mod Unsat	Modest	Likely	5.75	PAR			
24	Unsat	Sub	Unlikely	5.25	PAR			
16.5	Sat	Sub	Likely	8.25	PCR			

(Table continues on the following page.)

| Table A.5c | | All Approved Tunisia Projects, Evaluated and Ongoing, as of December 18, 2002 (continue |

Approval FY	Exit FY	Project ID	Project name	Lending instrument type
Rural Sector (continued)				
1985	FY92	P005660	NW Agri. Production	Investment
1985	FY95	P005661	NATL. IRR. MGMT. IMP	Investment
1986	FY94	P005665	Gabes Irrigation	Investment
1988	FY96	P005683	Forestry	Investment
1988	FY92	P005703	AG.CR.BNT IV	Investment
1989	FY95	P005692	ASAL II	Adjustment
1990	FY97	P005727	Research and Extension	Investment
1993	FY01	P005725	Second Forestry Deve.	Investment
1994	FY01	P005721	Agriculture Sec. Inv.	Investment
1995	FY01	P005720	Rural Finance	Investment
Transport				
1982	FY92	P005647	Highways V	Investment
1984	FY93	P005658	Urban Transport II	Investment
1988	FY95	P005672	Highway Maint. & Re.	Investment
1969	1975	P005599	Second port project	Investment
1969	1976	P005600	Railway project	Investment
1971	1977	P005605	Highway project	Investment
1974	1980	P005614	Tunis district urban planning and public transport proj	Investment
1976	1983	P005621	Second highway project	Investment
1978	1986	P005628	Rural roads project	Investment
1980	1988	P005636	Fourth highway project	Investment
1980	1989	P005637	Third ports project	Investment
1998	12/31/2004	P043700	TN- Transport Sector Investment	Investment
2001	6/30/2006	P064082	TN- Transport Sector Investment	Investment
Urban Development				
1972	1981	P005611	Tourism infrastructure project	Investment
1974	1981	P005613	Hotel training project	Investment
1979	1986	P005630	Second urban development project	Investment
1983	FY93	P005652	Urban Dev. III	Investment
1987	FY95	P005668	Urban IV	Investment
1989	FY97	P005691	Fifth Urban	Investment
1993	FY99	P005687	Municipal Sec. Inv.	Investment
1997	6/30/2003	P046832	TN- Municipal Development II	Investment
2001	6/30/2007	P048825	TN- Cultural Heritage	Investment
2003	2/28/2003	P074398	TN- Municipal Development III Project	Investment
Water Supply and Sanitation				
1969	1977	P005601	National water supply project	Investment
1970	1977	P005603	Second water supply project	Investment

Commitment ($m)	Outcome	ID	Sustainability	APPI	Eval type	Latest DO	Latest IP	Latest risk rating
15	Unsat	Negl	Unlikely	3.75	PCR			
22	Mod. Sat	Modest	Likely	5.75	EVM			
27.7	Sat	Sub	Likely	8.25	PCR			
20	Sat	Modest	Uncertain	6.75	EVM			
30	Sat	Sub	Uncertain	7.75	PAR			
84	Sat	Modest	Likely	7.25	EVM			
17	Mod. Sat	Modest	Uncertain	6	ES			
61.7	Sat	High	Likely	8.25	ES			
118.5	Sat	Sub	Highly Likely	8.25	ES			
65	Unsat	Modest	Unlikely	4.25	ES			
35.5	Sat	Modest	Likely	7.25	PAR			
33	Sat	Modest	Likely	7.25	PCR			
63	Sat	Modest	Likely	7.25	EVM			
8.5	Sat	NR	NR		PAR			
17	Sat	NR	NR		PAR			
24	Sat	NR	NR		PAR			
18	Unsat	NR	NR		PCR			
28	Sat	NR	NR		PCR			
32	Sat	NR	NR		PAR			
36.5	Sat	Sub	Likely		PCR			
42.5	Sat	Modest	Likely		PCR			
50.0						Sat	Sat	Modest
37.6						Sat	Sat	Modest
24	Sat	NR	NR		PCR			
5.6	Sat	NR	NR		PCR			
19	Sat	NR	NR		PAR			
25	Sat	Modest	Uncertain	6.75	PAR			
30.2	Unsat	Neg	Uncertain	4	EVM			
58	Mod. Sat	Modest	Likely	5.75	EVM			
75	Sat	Sub	Likely	8.25	PAR			
80						Sat	Sat	Modest
17						Sat	Sat	Modest
78.4						Sat	Sat	Sub
15	Sat	NR	NR		PAR			
10.5	Sat	NR	NR		PAR			

(Table continues on the following page.)

| Table A.5c | | All Approved Tunisia Projects, Evaluated and Ongoing, as of December 18, 2002 (continue |

Approval FY	Exit FY	Project ID	Project name	Lending instrument type
Water Supply and Sanitation (continued)				
1974	1980	P005615	Third water supply project	Investment
1975	1983	P005618	Urban sewerage project	Investment
1977	1984	P005626	Fourth water supply project	Investment
1979	1988	P005631	Second urban sewerage project	Investment
1979	1984	P005632	Fifth water supply project	Investment
1983	FY93	P005653	Urban Sewerage III	Investment
1984	FY93	P005659	Rural Water Supply	Investment
1995	6/30/2003	P005680	TN-Water Supply and Sewerage	Investment
1997	12/31/2004	P005731	TN- Greater Tunis Sewerage	Investment
Social Protection				
1991	FY95	P005734	Employment & Training	Investment
1996	6/30/2003	P005745	TN- 2nd Employment and Training	Investment
2002	8/31/2008	P048315	TN- Protected Areas Management Project	Investment
Multisector				
1999	3/31/2004	P055814	TN- Export Development	Investment

Source: OED internal database.

Commitment ($m)	Outcome	ID	Sustainability	APPI	Eval type	Latest DO	Latest IP	Latest risk rating
23	Sat	NR	NR		PAR			
28	Sat	NR	NR		PCR			
21	Sati	NR	NR		PCR			
26.5	Sat	NR	Likely		PAR			
25	Sat	NR	NR		PCR			
34	Sat	Sub	Likely	8.25	PCR			
50	Sat	Sub	Likely	8.25	PCR			
58.0						Sat	Sat	Modest
60.0						Unsat.	Unsat.	Sub
12	Sat	Sub	Uncertain	7.75	PAR			
60.0								
5.6								
35.0						Sat	Sat	Modes

ANNEX A.6: COST OF BANK PROGRAMS FOR TUNISIA AND COMPARATOR COUNTRIES

Table A.6a Costs				
Regions/countries	**Lending completion costs, $m**	**Supervision costs, $m**	**ESW completion costs, $m**	**Total costs, $m**
Bankwide	757.7	897.9	415	2,292
MNA	58.2	64.6	38	178
Tunisia	**9.8**	**9.3**	**4**	**24**
Algeria	5.8	8.1	3	21
Egypt, Rep. of	9.3	10.1	5	29
Jordan	7.8	6.2	3	19
Morocco	13.5	13.3	8	39
Percentages				
Bankwide	33%	39%	18%	90%
MNA	33%	36%	21%	91%
Tunisia	**40%**	**38%**	**16%**	**95%**
Algeria	28%	40%	17%	84%
Egypt, Rep. of	33%	35%	16%	100%
Jordan	42%	34%	15%	91%
Morocco	35%	34%	20%	89%

Table A.6b   Efficiency

Regions/countries	Total costs, $m	Number of projects	Net commit-ments, ($ million)	Net commitment for satisfactory & non-risky projects ($ million)	Average project size ($ million)	Average costs per project ($1,000)	Average costs ($s per $1,000 of net commitment)	Average costs ($s per $1,000 of net commitment for satisfactory & non-risky projects)
Bankwide	2,292	2,229	197,103	144,120	88	1,028	12	16
MNA	178	169	11,773	8,490	70	1,050	15	21
Tunisia	**24**	**27**	**1,888**	**1,810**	**70**	**900**	**13**	**13**
Algeria	21	19	1,967	1,218	104	1,079	10	17
Egypt, Rep. of	29	26	1,945	1,483	75	1,100	15	19
Jordan	19	19	864	724	45	974	21	26
Morocco	39	34	2,699	1,570	79	1,138	14	25

Note: The amount of total costs includes lending completion costs, supervision, scheduled and unscheduled ESW, and dropped project costs. The amount of lending completion costs includes lending completion costs and dropped project costs. The amount of ESW preparation costs includes unscheduled and scheduled ESW preparation costs.

Source: World bank database.

ANNEX A.7:   COUNTRY STRATEGY OBJECTIVES AND KEY INDICATORS

Table A.7a	1996 and 2000 Country Strategy Objectives and Key Macroeconomic and Structural Reform Performance Indicators

	Instruments	
Objectives	**AAA**	**Lending**
• Keep inflation under control	Private Sector Assessment Update (FY01); Social and Structural Review (FY00); Strategy for Public Debt Management (FY02); Export Growth: Determinants and Prospects (FY95); Private Sector Assessment (FY95); Towards the 21st Century (FY96)	ECAL I, II, III ($486m); Export Development ($35m); Transport Sector Investment I and II ($87.6m and $50m); Private Investment Credit Project ($120m); Industry Support Institutions Upgrading Project ($38.7m); ($60m) Economic and Financial Reforms Support Loan Project ($130m); Public Enterprise Reform Loan Project ($130m)
• Maintain viable financial balances		
• Increase international reserves		
• Sustained growth of real GDP		
• Strengthening private investment		
• Improve financial sector		
• Promote trade and openness		

Note: The early 1990s country strategy was not a stand-alone document as it was embedded in a loan document; it did not develop quantitative performance indicators for monitoring results.

a. The ratio for Algeria is 21%, Egypt 17%, and Morocco 23%..

b. World Development Indicators (Nov. 3, 2003), the ratio for Algeria is 0.3%, Egypt 0.5%, and Morocco 0.2%.

Source: Internal Bank data.

Proposed performance indicators for 1996–02	Actual progress
• Keep annual inflation at 3% during 1996-02, compared to 6% in 1995	• Annual inflation averaged about 3% during 1996-02
• Maintain fiscal deficit around 2% of GDP during 1996-02, down from 4% in 1995	• Fiscal deficit hovered around 3% of GDP during 1996-02
• Increase reserves to 3 months of imports, up from 2 months in 1995	• Gross foreign reserves rose to nearly 3 months of imports during 1996-02
• Sustain an annual GDP growth averaging 5-6% during 1996-02, up from 4% during 1991-95	• GDP growth accelerated to 5.6% over 1996-02
• Increase private investment to 15.4% of GDP by 2002, compared to 12% over 1990-96	• Private investment/GDP averaged 13.5% over 1997-02[a]
• Increase private investment to 56 percent of total investment by 2002, compared to 46 percent in 1995	• Private investment/total investment accounted for 56% in 2002
• Increase privatization proceeds (% of GDP) to 6% by 1999, compared to 1-2% in 1995	• Privatization proceeds/GDP accumulated to 9%
• Private sector banks as percentage of bank assets >50 percent in 1999, >60 percent in 2002, up from 30% in 1995	• Private bank assets/ total bank assets accounted for only 55% in 2002
• Increase ratio of Trade/PPP GDP >26 by 2002	• Trade (% of PPP GDP) reached 25.7
• Increase FDI/ PPP GDP > 0.7 by 2002	• Gross FDI (% of PPP GDP) amounted to 1.3%[b]

Table A.7b	1996 and 2000 Country Strategy Objectives and Key Human Development Performance Indicators	
	Instruments	
Objectives	**AAA**	**Lending**
• Achieve near universal primary education • Improve completion rates in education • Increase insertion rate of vocational graduates into workforce • Improvements in teacher training and qualifications • Reduce unemployment • Enhance financial sustainability of higher education • Reduce infant mortality • Lower fertility • Reduction in subsidized health care provision • Enhance the quality of health services • Improve the efficiency of health services • Ensure the sustainability of the health system	Social and Structural Review (FY00); Higher Education: Challenges and Opportunities (FY97)	Training and Employment Project II ($60m); Secondary Education Support Project ($98.3m); Higher Education Restructuring Project I ($75m); Higher Education Restructuring Project II ($50m); Employment and Training Fund Project ($12m); Education Quality Improvement Program Project ($99m); Health Sector Loan ($50m); Hospital Restructuring Support Project ($30m); Education and Training Sector Loan ($95m); Population and Family Health Project ($12m)

a. Government data "Statistiques de l' Enseignement Scolaire et de la Formation Professionnelle 2002-2003."

b. Internal Bank data.

Proposed performance indicators	Actual progress
• Net primary enrollment ratio of 100%	• 98.2% in 2000
• Raise persistence rate to grade 9 from 42% to 73% by 2004	• Completion rates for grades 6 and 7 were 87% and 63.5%, respectively, in 2001/2002[a]
• Placement rate of 60% for vocational graduates in 1999	• Monitoring system of placement of graduates into labor market set up and operational in 1998
• Reduce unemployment rate to 15% by 2002	• Unemployment at 14.9% in 2002
• Lower maternal mortality ratios	• Infant mortality at 26 per thousand in 2002
• Reduce infant mortality rate to 20 per thousand live births by 2002	• 8% of population have fully subsidized access and another 22% pay only 20% of the cost
• Lower subsidized health care availability to roughly 25% of the population in 1999	• MMR at 69 per 100,000 in 2002
• Improve health service quality through improved case management and staff training	• Hospital stay lowered from 8 to 7 days
• Policy measures for cost control	• At the regional health level, expenses recovered from Social Insurance program improved to 62.5% in 2003 from 2.2% in 1998; central government subsidy to recurrent budget of tertiary hospitals decreased to 35% (1998) from 69% (1991)[b]

Annex A.8	Tunisia: Task Manager Turnover in Projects Approved in FY90–03					
Project name	No. of changes (FY90-03)	**FY98**	**FY99**	**FY00**	**FY01**	**FY02**
Economic and Financial						
Export Development Project	0	a	a	a	a	a
Industry Support Institutions Upgrading	3	a	a	a	b	b
Private Investment Credit	4	a	a	b	b	b
Education						
Education Quality Improvement Program	2	a	a	a	b	b
Higher Education Reform Support II	1	a	a	a	b	b
Training and Employment II	1	a	a	a	a	b
Education Support II	1	a	a	b	b	b
Higher Education Restructuring	2	a	a	a	b	b
Environment, Energy, and Mining						
Gas Infrastructure Development Project	0	a	a	a	a	a
Health, Nutrition and Population						
Health Sector Loan	1	a	a	a	b	b
Hospital Restructuring Support	5	a	a	b	b	b
Population and Family Health	1	a	a	a	a	a
Rural Sector						
Northwest Mount. and Forestry Areas Dev.	1	a	a	a	a	a
Agricultural Support Services	1	a	a	a	a	b
Water Sector Investment Loan	2	a	a	a	b,c	c
Second Agricultural Sector Investment	1	a	a	b	b	b
Natural Resources Management	2	a	a	b	b	c
National Rural Finance	2	a	a	b,c	c	c
Agricultural Sector Investment Loan	1	a	b	b	b	b
Northwest Mountainous Areas Dev.	2	a	b	b	b	b
Second Forestry Development	2	a	a	b	b	b
Transport						
Transport Sector Investment I	0	a	a	a	a	a
Rural Roads	2	b	c	c	c	c
Urban Development and Water Supply and Sanitation						
Municipal Development III	1	a	a	a	a	a
Cultural Heritage	0	a	a	a	a	a
Municipal Development II	3	a	b,c	c	d	d
Municipal Sector Investment	4	a	b,c,d	d	d	d
Greater Tunis Sewerage Project	3	a	a	b	b	c,d
Water Supply and Sewerage	3	a	a	b	b	c,d
Adjustment						
ECAL III	0	a	a	a	a	a
ECAL II	1	a	a	a	a	b
ECAL I	2	a	a	a	a	a
Economic and Financial Ref. Supp. Loan	1	a	a	a	a	a

Note: a = no change since FY98; b = one change since FY98; c = two changes since FY98; d = three changes since FY98.
Source: World Bank project data.

Annex A.9	Tunisia: Bank's Senior Management, 1991–03		
Year	**Vice president**	**Country director**	**Resident representative**
1991	Willi A. Wapenhans	Kemal Dervis	-
1992	Caio Koch-Weser	Pieter P. Bottelier	-
1993	Caio Koch-Weser	Harinder S. Kohli	-
1994	Caio Koch-Weser	Daniel Ritchie	-
1995	Caio Koch-Weser	Daniel Ritchie	-
1996	Kemal Dervis	Daniel Ritchie	-
1997	Kemal Dervis	Christian Delvoie	-
1998	Kemal Dervis	Christian Delvoie	-
1999	Kemal Dervis	Christian Delvoie	-
2000	Jean-Louis Sarbib	Christian Delvoie	-
2001	Jean-Louis Sarbib	Christian Delvoie	-
2002	Jean-Louis Sarbib	Theodore O. Ahlers	-
2003	Christiaan J. Poortman	Theodore O. Ahlers	-

Source: World Bank Group Directory.

ANNEX B: LIST OF PEOPLE MET ON MISSION IN TUNISIA (AND WORLD BANK AND IMF STAFF INTERVIEWED)

Government Officials, Donors, and Private Sector Representatives

Ministry of Development & International Cooperation
Kamel Ben Rejeb, Director General
Monir Boumessouer, Director General, Infrastructure
Fouad El Shrafi, Director
Lutfi Frad, Director
Mohamed Naceur Braham, Counselor of Public Services, Director of Agriculture and Agro-Industries
Foued Charfi, Director General, Productive Sectors
Borgi Kacem, Director General of Regional Development
Abel Hamid Triki, Director
Moncef Youzbachi

Ministry of Finance
Belhadji Jameleddine, Director General

Ministry of Higher Education
Abdallah Riahi, Director, Studies and Planning
Mohamed El Hedi Zaiem, Consultant

Ministry of Education and Formation and Institute of Training
H. E. Mohamed El-Monsif Ben Saad, Government Secretary General (Deputy Minister)
Abdelkader Lgoulli, Director General, Services
Abdelmalik Elsallami, Advisor to the Minister
Ahmed Midamia, Director General, NVC
Mohamed Nazar El-Aish, Director General
Farahat El-Nasiri, Director
Mohamed El-Nasir, Director

Ibrahim Eltoumi, Director
Lutfi Blzabis, Director
Hofia El-Bahri, Director

Ministry of Health
Dr. Khaled Kheireddine, Director of Planning
Slaheddine Kalat, Director of Equipments
Nacer Kamel, Director of Studies

National Statistical Institute
Khalifa Ben Faqih, Director General
Abdel Majd El-Wislati

Tunisia Central Bank
Habib El Montacer, Managing Director
Badreddine Barkia, Director General, Supervision
Samir Brahimi, Director General, Services & Audit

Ministry of Transport
Salem Miladi, Director General

Ministry of Industry and Energy
Hamdi Guezguez, Principal Engineer
Ridha Ben Mosbah, Director General, De mise à niveaù
Mohamed El Kamel, Project Manager, ISIUP

Private Sector
Noureddine Ferchiou, Advocat, Ferchio Assoices
Ahmed Benghazi, Associe-Gérant, Axis
Ahmed Smaoui
Prof. Marouanne El Abassi
Faycal Lakhoua, Counsellor, IACE
Jurgen Blanken, Water Sector Economist, Private Consultant

National Agricultural Bank

Berraies Mohamed, Directeur

Exports Promotion Agency (FAMEX)

Slim Chaker, Director for Coordination

Trade Union

Mohamed Trabelsi, Secretaire

AfDB

O. Ojo, Chief Evaluation Officer

K. Diallo, Principal Economist

EU

Bernard Brunet, Premier Secrètaire

Manfredo Fanti, Premier Secrètaire

Paul Mathieu, Economist

Philippe Massin, Rural Development Expert

Amparo Gonzalez Diez, Section Chief, Rural Development and the Environment

Jose-Maria Bellostas, Rural Development Expert

Tunisia Leasing

Fethi Mestri, Director General

Ministry of Agriculture, Environment and Water Resources

Ahmed El Achek, President Director General, Office of Sylvo-Pastoral Development of the North West

Badr Ben Ammar, General Rural Economist, Director General of Studies and Agricultural Development

Abderraman Chaffai, Director, Studies and Agricultural Development

Ahmed Ridha Fekih Salem, General Engineer, Director General of Forests

Mohamed Gharbi, Director General, Agricultural Land Agency

Abdellatif Ghedira, Chief of Mission, Cabinet of the Minister, Director of the Bureau of Planning and Hydraulics

Lamine Ben Hamadi, Deputy Director of Planning and Budget, Institute of Research and Higher Learning

Mohamed Ben Hamouda, Teacher-Researcher, Coordinator of Regional Research Pole of the Northwest, Institute of Research and Higher Learning

Mohamed Mounir Hedri, Director of Research Institute of Research and Higher Learning

Said Helal, Chief Engineer, Water and Forests, Director of Socio-Economic Development of the Forest Population

Abdelkadar Hamdane, Director General of Rural Works and of Hydraulics

Abdallah Mallek, Director General of Finance, Investment and Professional Organisations

Bellakhal Moktar, Director of Agriculture Extension

Kachouri Mondher, Deputy Director of Monitoring & Evaluation of Research Programs, Institute of Research and Higher Learning

Sahla Mezghani, Agro-economist, Section Chief, Finance, Investment, and Professional Organizations

Ben Mohamed Mongi, Chief, General Laboratory, Director of Tuniso Japanese Project

Abdelaziz Mougou, President, Institute of Research and Higher Learning

Hamda Zeramdini, Agriculture Extension and Training Agency, Coordinator of the Agriculture Support Services Project

World Bank, IMF, and Islamic Development Bank Staff

Theodore O. Ahlers (Country Director)

Christian Delvoie (then Country Director)

Dimmitri Vittas (Senior Adviser, OPD)

Daniel Ritchie (then COD Division Chief)

John Page (Director, PRMPR)

Aristomene Varoudakis (Country Economist)

Cecile Fruman (Country Officer)

Pedro Alba (Sector Manager, MNSED)

Mustapha Nabli (Chief Economist and Director, MNSED)

Setareh Razmara (Senior Economist, MNSHD)

Sara Johansson (Economist, MNSED)

Hamid Alavi (Senior Private Sector Development Specialist, MNSIF)

Jeffery Waite (Senior Education Specialist, MNSHD)

Meskerem Mulatu (Senior Education Specialist, AFTH2)

Anwar Bach-Baouab (Lead Operations Officer, AFTH3)
Gillian Perkins (Consultant OEDST)
Domenico Fanizza (Deputy Division Chief, IMF)
Bader Elddine Nouioua, Advisor, Operations Evaluation Office, Islamic Development Bank
Djelloula Saci, Head, Operations Evaluation Office, Islamic Development Bank
Abdel Ouahab Ghazala, Operations Evaluation Office, Islamic Development Bank

ANNEX C: GUIDE TO OED'S COUNTRY ASSISTANCE EVALUATION METHODOLOGY

This methodological note describes the key elements of OED's Country Assistance Evaluation (CAE) methodology.[1]

CAEs rate the outcomes of Bank assistance programs, not clients' overall development progress.

An assistance program needs to be assessed on how well it met its particular objectives, which are typically a sub-set of the client's development objectives. If an assistance program is large in relation to the client's total development effort, the program outcome will be similar to the client's overall development progress. However, most Bank assistance programs provide only a fraction of the total resources devoted to a client's development by donors, stakeholders, and the government itself. In CAEs, OED rates only the outcome of the Bank's program, not the client's overall development outcome, although the latter is clearly relevant for judging the program's outcome.

The experience gained in CAEs confirms that program outcomes sometimes diverge significantly from the client's overall development progress. CAEs have identified assistance programs that had:

- Satisfactory outcomes matched by good client development
- Unsatisfactory outcomes with clients that achieved good overall development results, notwithstanding the weak Bank program
- Satisfactory outcomes with clients that did not achieve satisfactory overall results during the period of program implementation.

Assessments of assistance program outcome and Bank performance are not the same.

By the same token, an unsatisfactory assistance program outcome does not always mean that

Bank performance was also unsatisfactory, and *vice-versa*. This becomes clearer once we consider that the Bank's contribution to the outcome of its assistance program is only part of the story. The assistance program's outcome is determined by the *joint* impact of four agents: (a) the client, (b) the Bank, (c) partners and other stakeholders, and (d) exogenous forces (such as events of nature, international economic shocks, and so on). Under the right circumstances, a negative contribution from any one agent might overwhelm the positive contributions from the other three, and lead to an unsatisfactory outcome.

OED measures Bank performance primarily on the basis of contributory actions the Bank directly controlled. Judgments regarding Bank performance typically consider the relevance and implementation of the strategy; the design and supervision of the Bank's lending interventions; the scope, quality, and follow-up of diagnostic work and other analytical and advisory activities; the consistency of the Bank's lending with its nonlending work and with its safeguard policies; and the Bank's partnership activities.

Evaluation in Three Dimensions

As a check on the inherent subjectivity of ratings, OED examines a number of elements that contribute to assistance program outcomes. The consistency of ratings is further tested by examining the country assistance program across three dimensions:

(a) A *Products and Services Dimension,* involving a "bottom-up" analysis of major program inputs—loans, analytical and advisory activities, and aid coordination

(b) A *Development Impact Dimension,* involving a "top-down" analysis of the principal program objectives for relevance, efficacy, outcome, sustainability, and institutional impact

(c) An *Attribution Dimension,* in which the evaluator assigns responsibility for the program outcome to the four categories of actors.

Rating Assistance Program Outcome

In rating the outcome (expected development impact) of an assistance program, OED gauges the extent to which major strategic objectives were relevant and achieved, without any shortcomings. Programs typically express their goals in terms of higher-order objectives, such as poverty reduction. The Country Assistance Strategy (CAS) may also establish intermediate goals, such as improved targeting of social services or promotion of integrated rural development, and specify how they are expected to contribute toward achieving the higher-order objective. OED's task is then to validate whether the intermediate objectives produced satisfactory net benefits and whether the results chain specified in the CAS was valid. Where causal linkages were not fully specified in the CAS, it is the evaluator's task to reconstruct this causal chain from the available evidence and assess relevance, efficacy, and outcome with reference to the intermediate and higher-order objectives.

Evaluators also assess the degree of client ownership of international development priorities, such as the Millennium Development Goals, and Bank corporate advocacy priorities, such as safeguards. Ideally, any differences in dealing with these issues would be identified and resolved by the CAS, enabling the evaluator to focus on whether the tradeoffs adopted were appropriate. However, in other instances, the strategy may be found to have glossed over certain conflicts or avoided addressing key client development constraints. In either case, the consequences could include a diminution of program relevance, a loss of client ownership, and/or unwelcome side-effects, such as safeguard violations, all of which must be taken into account in judging program outcome.

Ratings Scale

OED utilizes six rating categories for **outcome**, ranging from highly satisfactory to highly unsatisfactory:

Highly Satisfactory: The assistance program achieved at least acceptable progress toward all major relevant objectives, **and** had best practice development impact on one or more of them. No major shortcomings were identified**.**

Satisfactory: The assistance program achieved acceptable progress toward all major relevant objectives. No best practice achievements or major shortcomings were identified**.**

Moderately Satisfactory: The assistance program achieved acceptable progress toward *most* of its major relevant objectives. No major shortcomings were identified.

Moderately Unsatisfactory: The assistance program did *not* make acceptable progress toward *most* of its major relevant objectives, *or* made acceptable progress on all of them, but either (a) did not take into adequate account a key development constraint or (b) produced a major shortcoming, such as a safeguard violation.

Unsatisfactory: The assistance program did not make acceptable progress toward *most* of its major relevant objectives, *and* either (a) did not take into adequate account a key development constraint or (b) produced a major shortcoming, such as a safeguard violation.

Highly Unsatisfactory: The assistance program did not make acceptable progress toward *any* of its major relevant objectives and did not take into adequate account a key development constraint, while also producing at least one major shortcoming, such as a safeguard violation.

The **institutional development impact (IDI)** can be rated as: *high*, *substantial*, *modest*, or *negligible*. IDI measures the extent to which the program bolstered the client's ability to make more efficient, equitable, and sustainable use of its human, financial, and natural resources. Examples of areas included in judging the institutional development impact of the program are:

- The soundness of economic management
- The structure of the public sector and, in particular, the civil service
- The institutional soundness of the financial sector
- The soundness of legal, regulatory, and judicial systems

- The extent of monitoring and evaluation systems
- The effectiveness of aid coordination
- The degree of financial accountability
- The extent of building NGO capacity
- The level of social and environmental capital.

Sustainability can be rated as *highly likely*, *likely*, *unlikely*, *highly unlikely*, or, if available information is insufficient, *non-evaluable*. Sustainability measures the resilience to risk of the development benefits of the country assistance program over time, taking into account eight factors:

- Technical resilience
- Financial resilience (including policies on cost recovery)

- Economic resilience
- Social support (including conditions subject to safeguard policies)
- Environmental resilience
- Ownership by governments and other key stakeholders
- Institutional support (including a supportive legal/regulatory framework, and organizational and management effectiveness)
- Resilience to exogenous effects, such as international economic shocks or changes in the political and security environments.

ANNEX D: MANAGEMENT ACTION RECORD

Major Monitorable OED Recommendations Requiring a Response	Management Response
• *Follow through on supporting programs to improve the environment for private sector development and enhance competitiveness* as Tunisia seeks to integrate within the world economy. Specifically, the Bank should help the country (i) pursue trade openness with the EU and the rest of the world; (ii) improve the enabling environment through regulatory and judicial reforms to attract private and foreign investment; and (iii) progress on privatizing public financial and enterprise firms.	The proposed CAS for FY05-08 addresses these issues squarely. The first pillar of the CAS focuses on improving the business environment and enhancing competitiveness, while the second pillar supports greater quality and efficiency of the education system to address the needs of the market place. The CAS supports greater competition in infrastructure through the PPI (private participation in infrastructure) agenda.
• *Continue support for social sectors.* While supportive of the MDGs, the Bank's program needs to continue this emphasis and focus on improving the country's capacity to prioritize social spending and address education expansion at the post-basic level, given the demographic transition under way. The Bank should undertake a public expenditure review in partnership with the government. This should help build capacity to prioritize social spending and provide the basis for measures to efficiently address growing demand for secondary and tertiary education.	This is also addressed in the new CAS though the second pillar (education), and the third pillar, which supports greater efficiency of social programs (pension, health, and social protection). A PER is proposed and the country team agrees that emphasis should be given to reviewing expenditures in social sectors.
• *Focus on institutional development and safety nets in the rural sector.* Future Bank programs should focus on rural institutional development to support efficient output and input markets, including land, rural finance, and research and extension, while maintaining social cohesion through better targeted safety nets. After 21 years without a comprehensive agricultural sector review, the Bank should undertake one to inform its future programs.	The Country Team has taken the CAE's recommendation and proposes to conduct a comprehensive agricultural sector review. This will inform policy dialogue and future lending to this sector.
• *Enhance a results-based monitoring and evaluation approach.* Enhancing a results-based approach with agreed and monitorable output and outcome indicators embedded in an improved monitoring and evaluation framework would help to anchor the Bank's assistance program in the future.	The proposed FY05-08 CAS is a results-based CAS and will lead to regular monitoring of CAS outcomes and results (yearly reports and a CAS progress report in 2006). In addition, the country team has already started reinforcing capacity of project implementation staff in Tunisia in regular M&E of projects. CB will also be strengthened for Bank teams.

Executive Summary

The Operations Evaluation Office (OEO) of the Islamic Development Bank (IDB) has recently embarked on new areas of operations evaluation, such as country assistance evaluation, sector or thematic studies, and impact evaluation. The second Country Assistance Evaluation (CAE) was conducted by OEO for Tunisia in September 2003 in collaboration with the World Bank's Operations Evaluation Department (OED)—the first being the CAE conducted for Jordan in October 2002. The main objective of the CAE is to assess the relevance and effectiveness of IDB's interventions in Tunisia since the start of IDB operations in 1976. The scope of the present CAE report is limited to the Bank's project financing activities.

Regarding its economy in general, the determined structural reforms in Tunisia led to markedly improving economic and social performance. Real GDP growth increased from 2.8 percent during 1982–86 to 4.8 percent during 1991–2001. Meanwhile, both inflation and the current account deficit decreased significantly. The 2002 GPD growth was reported to have decelerated sharply due to the combined effect of the aftermath of September 11, 2001, and a severe 4-year drought. The growth outlook for 2003 appears to be highly imperiled by several risky parameters. It is estimated to stand at around 4 percent, owing to the sluggish recovery of traditional export markets to the European Union (EU) and the slight recovery from the drought. However, the main factor of challenge for the Tunisian economy in the near future, especially for its industry, is definitely whether it can stand up to the expected competition when the free trade agreement with the European Union will come into force in 2008.

During the 1970s and 1980s, IDB's strategy for development assistance to Tunisia was mainly targeted to developing the industrial sector (mainly through equity participation), the public utilities sector (potable water supply and sanitation), together with development in agriculture (including integrated rural development) in line with priorities of the government. In the 1990s, the IDB assistance programmes were mainly guided by the Country Assistance Strategy Study (CASS) prepared in 1996 for the period 1997–99 and the subsequent finalisation of a 3-year rolling work programme for the period 1420-1422H. The Bank's operations had sharply declined over the 3 years preceding the preparation of the CASS for Tunisia. The main reason was the availability of more competitive alternative financing sources, particularly from the EU and various bilateral donors. This really was a threat for more IDB involvement in Tunisia, especially since it has been categorized as a mid-high-income country and could not benefit any more from blending of concessional and non-concessional modes of financing.

By and large, IDB assistance to Tunisia has been diverse. The Bank assistance focused on public utilities; agriculture and rural development; industry; financial sector; and, more recently, on social sectors (education and health). As of June 2003, the IDB has approved a total amount of US$1.18 billion for Tunisia, 70 percent of which is for trade operations. Out of 44 ordinary project financing operations, 20 operations are currently active while 24 operations have already been completed. The total amount actually disbursed by the Bank for projects and technical assistance operations up to mid-2003 was ID 94.48 million, or around one-third of the net approved amount. This low figure implies partially that there has been under-utilisation of the extended financings as there were many cost savings that stemmed from both the depreciation of the Tunisian dinar and a tendency to overestimate the project costs at appraisal time.

With regard to the performance of the 11 post-evaluated projects, 10 projects were considered as successful or partly successful, and one project not successful. Currently, a 3-year work programme for 1423-1425H is being implemented as planned.

During two decades (1980s and 1990s), Tunisia's commitments in trade were almost constant and in line with earmarked allocations, thanks to annual operations entered into with traditional clients in that member country.

However, it is felt that Tunisia has not been engaging with the IDB on trade financing operations at a level that is commensurate with the high creditworthiness that the country enjoys. The main reason Tunisia does not take advantage of the IDB's trade financing operations, at a similar pace to other member countries of comparable economic development, is that IDB's mark-up is perceived—particularly by the private sector—not to be competitive enough compared with the rates available.

Water supply and sanitation has been the primary beneficiary sector of IDB project financing (45 percent), with particular emphasis on the construction of sewerage infrastructure in favour of the Sewerage Authority (ONAS). Under IDB financing, ONAS procured new technology of sludge mechanical dewatering and handling. Regarding the water supply, two projects are currently being implemented by the Water Authority (SONEDE). In view of the relatively low rate of access to potable water of northern zones, IDB may envisage in the future to finance projects in these regions. It was proposed also that IDB might contribute to the SONEDE programme of renewal of transmission lines in urban areas.

IDB assistance to the industrial sector was primarily provided in the early 1980s through equity participation in three companies. The CAE mission recommends to undertake a review of the equity portfolio performance in Tunisia, in light of the difficulties faced by these companies.

The Bank's intervention in the Integrated Rural Development (IRD) sector related to 5 projects that entailed activities that were spread all over Tunisia, and whose scope encompassed a multitude of components of both agricultural and nonagricultural nature. All the 5 IRD projects have been post evaluated, and their performance was assessed as satisfactory since the targeted objectives were attained in terms of regional development and improvement of the living conditions of the most disfavoured populations.

IDB involvement in the social sectors has been rather modest and tardy. Although the human resources development was a top priority for Tunisia, IDB was involved neither in primary and secondary education nor in vocational training. IDB involvement in higher education and the health sector is relatively recent, and it is premature to assess its performance.

With regard to education, many stakeholders interviewed by the mission expressed high concern about the lagging improvements in the quality of education at all levels. For higher education in particular, the Tunisian officials informed the mission that their country is putting more emphasis on vocational and technical education, especially computers and information technology, to combat unemployment among the youth, which now stands at around 16 percent. In this connection, the Ministry in charge of higher education is preparing a project to create technological poles, and IDB may envisage its contribution to this project.

On the other hand, IDB extended several lines of financing to Tunisia, but most of them have remained dormant. The main reason for the non-utilization of these lines of financing is the foreign exchange risk which the local investors and businessmen are unwilling to bear. In this respect, a new global line was approved in 2003. It has been devised to overcome all the shortcomings related to previous lines of financing extended to local banks in Tunisia, especially through the introduction of a mechanism for the exchange risk coverage, involving local banks and insurance companies.

In conclusion, the Tunisian authorities affirmed the importance and the timeliness of the current evaluation of IDB's activities in Tunisia. The IDB's assistance to Tunisia has been appreciated and acknowledged by them. There was a general agreement that this assistance was relevant. As a matter of fact, IDB's experience in dealing with the different executing agencies is considered very successful, because Tunisia possesses a very efficient and experienced technical and administrative staff. However, there were a number of criticisms of bank assistance. The complaints concern mainly operational aspects such as time-consuming disbursement procedures and IDB financing cost, which is viewed to be rather high.

ATTACHMENT 2: REPORT FROM THE COMMITTEE ON DEVELOPMENT EFFECTIVENESS (CODE)

The Informal Subcommittee (SC) of the Committee on Development Effectiveness (CODE) met on April 21, 2004, to discuss the Tunisia Country Assistance Evaluation prepared jointly by the Operations Evaluation Department (OED) and the Islamic Development Bank (IDB).

Background

OED's evaluation commended Tunisia's remarkable socioeconomic progress and reduction in poverty rates and underlined the important role of country ownership, a broad political consensus, a well-developed human resource base, and a stable macroeconomic environment. The report noted that the Bank program in Tunisia succeeded in promoting reforms in the financial, rural, and private sectors by providing assistance in terms of policy advice, lending, and resource mobilization. It also noted some shortfalls that may pose risks for sustaining high performance in the more competitive environment that Tunisia is likely to face in the near future, such as low levels of private investment, the significant role of government in economic activities, the large number of nonperforming loans at public banks, and high tariffs. The evaluation concluded that the Bank should concentrate its efforts on helping the authorities to improve the business environment through regulatory reform, to continue support for the rural sector and social institutions, and on high-quality analytical studies.

Management broadly agreed with the CAE conclusions and noted that they will be largely reflected in the new Tunisia country strategy. In particular, the new country strategy will focus on three strategic objectives: (i) strengthening the environment for private investment; (ii) improving the quality of output from the education system and its link to the labor market; and (iii) improving public services through a focus on efficiency and sustainability of public expenditures.

The Chair representing Tunisia thanked OED for preparing a very balanced and insightful report, and reiterated the Tunisian authorities' general agreement with the main conclusions and recommendations of the evaluation. He concurred with the OED assessment of the Bank assistance as satisfactory, and highlighted the important role of the Bank's lending, policy advice and analytical work in the country's socioeconomic development. At the same time, he stressed that the authorities have employed a cautious approach to structural reforms in order to ensure a broad consensus. He also expressed concerns about the increasing pressure of the cost of doing business with the Bank and noted that the report could have benefited from drawing comparisons with other MDBs, as well as specific proposals to improve flexibility of the country strategy program and IFC's involvement in the country.

Main Conclusions and Next Steps

The Subcommittee welcomed the CAE and agreed with the OED rating of Bank assistance as satisfactory. Members endorsed the main conclusions and recommendations of the report. They commended management for including the CAE's recommendations in the new country strategy, and stressed the importance of drawing lessons from Tunisia's impressive performance. Among other major issues discussed at the meeting were the pace of future reforms, challenges of sustaining the development progress and related vulnerabilities of the Tunisian economy, the cost of doing business in Tunisia in the context of Bank lending to the middle-income countries, and the lessons to be drawn from the joint evaluations with other development partners.

The following points were raised:

Lessons Learned

Many members were interested in the positive lessons from the Tunisian experience, and whether they could be replicated in other countries. Management noted that Tunisian experience is very relevant, especially for the MNA and Africa Regions, and that it is being currently utilized through a series of Regional seminars and workshops. Some members asked for more details on the impact of and the differences in views on the *mise à niveau* program of enterprise restructuring and upgrading. Management noted that in its view the main factor in supporting enterprise restructuring should be the investment climate rather than providing a small amount of subsidy, which is the essence of the *mise à niveau* program

Looking Forward

Members concurred with the report's conclusion that the Bank should continue to support improving the investment climate and enhancing competitiveness. They stressed the importance of developing a results-based approach in the areas of trade openness, the business environment, enterprise and financial sector privatization, and land and rural finance. Members expressed concern about the size of the public banks' portfolio and potentially heavy burden of nonperforming loans on the economy. Some members concurred with OED's observation that further structural reforms are needed in light of an increasingly more competitive regional and global trade environment, but noted the importance of simultaneously sustaining full ownership of the reform process and broad political consensus. Management noted that there is interest on behalf of the authorities to take advantage of the Bank's assistance on debt management and doing an investment climate assessment. Some members asked about the reasons of IFC's lack of activity in the country. Management replied that IFC's limited involvement is due to the availability of alternative and cheaper financing for Tunisian companies. At the same time, management confirmed that IFC is interested in exploring new opportunities in Tunisia. Members praised the country's success in achieving the MDGs, but had questions about the consistently high levels of unemployment. Management agreed that, despite meeting the target on unemployment, job creation and private investment remain issues of concern for the Tunisian authorities, given the rapid growth of the labor force. Management noted that those issues are discussed extensively in the country strategy through the prism of creating more flexibility in public financial management and improving the investment climate. Some members asked management to elaborate on the absence of a full-fledged Bank office in the country. Management replied that given the presence of very strong and competent public administration, the Tunisian authorities at this point do not see the need for the same kind of implementation assistance as in other countries.

Cost of Doing Business

Some members echoed the concern expressed by the Tunisian chair about the cost of doing business with the Bank vis-à-vis other MDBs, and stressed the importance of that issue in the overall context of lending to the middle-income countries. OED noted that these issues will be addressed in the OED study on lending to middle-income countries. Management added that Tunisia could clearly be a case where the Bank can quickly adopt national systems in order to drive down the costs, and that the future work on core ESW (CFAA, CPAR) is designed to address fiduciary issues so as to move toward using national systems.

Donor Coordination

Members welcomed OED's cooperation with IDB, consistent with the Bank's broader agenda of harmonization and reducing the cost of assistance to the clients, and urged OED to continue that practice in future. Some members were interested to know whether joint work was an important factor in the overall success of the evaluation, and what were the lessons learned. OED replied that the partnership arrangement with IDB led to significant capacity development, laying the groundwork for further collaboration. This was the second joint report with IDB, and OED had found those exercises very useful in terms of raising the efficiency of the evaluation function, capacity building, and sharing of ideas. Management noted that the high level of competence of the Tunisian authorities allows for a sufficient level of dialogue with donors to be maintained bilaterally, but encouraged the authorities to do it in a more coordinated manner in the future.

Chander Mohan Vasudev, Chairman

ENDNOTES

Chapter 1

1. The GDI ranks Jordan 75th, Tunisia 76th, Algeria 88th, Egypt 99th, and Morocco 102nd out of 175 countries (UNDP 2003).

2. Deeper integration into EU markets will make Tunisia more vulnerable to economic swings in the EU. Anemic growth in the EU is swiftly felt in Tunisia, as in the sharp GDP slowdown seen in 2002.

Chapter 2

1. Most of the World Bank's closed projects in Tunisia do not have an operationalized M&E mechanism.

2. The Region notes, "It is important to indicate that it was not the Bank's choice not to conduct a PER but the Government's reluctance to let the Bank do one."

3. By way of comparison, only the Bank's West Bank and Gaza program mobilized more resources than Tunisia. During FY94–01, the West Bank and Gaza program secured $541 million in co-financing/parallel funding against $326 million in Bank commitments—a ratio of $1.66 on every dollar. The Bank's Jordan program mobilized a co-financing ratio similar to its program in Tunisia.

4. For example, Municipal Development Project was postponed and Cultural Heritage and Agricultural Support Services projects were reduced in size by 40 percent.

Chapter 3

1. The authorities noted that when these private leasing companies are combined with the private banks, the share of assets of all private credit institutions out of the total is about 62 percent.

2. Excludes five "development" banks that are joint ventures with other Arab countries (which account for about 5 percent of the banking assets) and are not subject to the authority and supervision of the Central Bank, but are governed by bilateral protocols. These are now being commercialized and the intention is to bring them under the umbrella of the Central Bank. Three foreign banks operate in Tunisia today, BNP, Citibank, and *Société Générale*, and the Arab Banking Group has recently been authorized to open up a branch as well. However, the presence of foreign banks in Tunisia remains below that seen in other developing countries, especially in EU accession countries that have modernized their banking systems with a significant involvement of foreign banks.

3. The reduction in NPLs was largely the result of the government taking over or guaranteeing bad debts rather than evidence of better lending.

4. In 2002, average (unweighted) Tunisian most favored nation (MFN) tariffs were 34.5 percent, marginally down from 35.9 in 2000, compared with 24.3 percent for imports originating in the EU.

5. FDI flows also account for only a small percentage of gross capital formation in the region, about 5 percent in 2000. In comparison, FDI flows accounted for 26 percent in Singapore (World Bank data, 2003).

6. Tunisia's unemployment rate is similar to the MNA average of 15 percent in 2000 (*Finance and Development*, March 2003, p. 19). Based on its ESW, the Bank has proposed measures to improve the unemployment situation.

7. The Bank's first education project in Tunisia was in 1962.

8. Government data, *Statistiques de l'enseignement scolaire*, 2002–03.

9. Third International Mathematics and Science Study measured student performance in mathematics and science achievements and collected relevant information on instruction, curriculum, schools, and policies.

10. The ongoing Education Quality Improvement Program Phase 1 (EQIP 1). See Annex table A-2o.

11. Hospital Restructuring Support Project of 1991.

12. The Region notes that there has been substantial progress on the reforms concerning the Regional health bodies, although it was slow until about two years ago. OED notes that the Region, in its evaluation of the health structuring project, mentioned that requiring a legal framework for hospital autonomy as a condition for project effectiveness is important to ensure political commitment.

13. According to the Ministry of Education projections covering the period 2000–20, secondary education student numbers will increase by 80 percent and basic education students will decrease by 40 percent.

14. Tunisia's expenditure per student rises sharply with the level of education. For example, per capita tertiary spending is five times higher than primary level and three times higher than secondary spending. These ratios do not compare favorably with comparator countries (World Bank data, 2003).

15. Economic and fiscal analyses are light in the context of this program.

16. This section draws heavily on World Bank (2003) and Tsakok (2004).

17. These objectives addressed all issues the Bank raised in its analytical work except the high risks of a drought-vulnerable agriculture and the weaknesses of marketing. The Bank addressed the growth, sustainability, and poverty reduction objectives of the government, but did not pay sufficient attention in its program to the government's other major objectives of achieving food self-sufficiency and increasing rural employment.

18. The 1995 EUAA excludes agricultural goods. However, an agricultural agreement with the EU in January 2001 presented new opportunities for Tunisian exports, which would boost the country's position in the European market, especially for products such as olive oil, double-concentrate tomato paste, and table grapes.

19. The center west is the poorest, according to the Bank data. In the Natural Resources Management project (1997–03) operating in the north (Jendouba), center west (Kasserine), and south (Medenine), there have been substantial physical achievements, but since there is no M&E, there is no systematic evidence on the income-increasing impact, which is presumed to be positive.

20. World Bank. Tunisia Northwest Mountainous Ares Development project report.

21. A proposed policy note on land issues (mentioned in the 2000 CAS) was dropped.

22. Tunisia has successfully diversified its exports toward new manufactured products, including electrical machinery, tobacco, footwear, explosives, and pyrotechnics (World Bank 2000b), p. 14.

Chapter 4

1. One exception is the 1993 PERL. The project seems to have been too ambitious and unrealistic in its design from the onset. It was the first operation to try to help a reluctant country deal with the difficult area of public enterprise reform, employing an experimental instrument embodied in the performance contracts, and resorting to imprecise conditionalities that started weak and got weaker during implementation. It was also poorly supervised, except for its transport component.

REFERENCES

Adams, Richard, and John Page. 2003. "Poverty, Inequality and Growth in Selected Middle East and North Africa Countries, 1980–2003." *World Development* 13 (12): 2027–48.

Ayadi, Mohamed, Mohamed Salah Matoussi, and Maria Victoria-Feser. 2001."Putting Robust Statistical Methods into Practice: Poverty Analysis in Tunisia." *Swiss Journal of Economics and Statistics* 137 (3) 463–82.

Dabour, Nabil. 2000. "The Role of Foreign Direct Investment in Development and Growth in OIC Member Countries." *Journal of Economic Cooperation* 21 (3).

IMF (International Monetary Fund). 2003. *Tunisia—Preliminary Conclusions of the Article IV Consultation Mission for 2003.* Washington, D.C.

Kanaan, A. 2004. "Evaluating Bank Assistance in the Areas of Macroeconomic Management, Private Sector Development and Financial Sector Development." OED Working Paper. Washington, D.C.

OECD (Organisation for Economic Co-operation and Development). 2003. "Geographical Distribution of Financial Flow Aid Recipients." Paris.

Tsakok, I. 2004. "Rural Development and Poverty Reduction 1990-2003." OED Working Paper. Washington, D.C.

Tunisia, Ministry of Economic Development (MED). 2002. *The Tenth Plan: 2002–06.* Tunis.

———. 1997. *Ninth Plan: 1997–01.* Tunis.

Tunisia, Ministry of Development and International Cooperation, National Institute of Statistics. 2000. *National Survey on Household Budget, Consumption, and Living Standards–2000.* Volume A. *Results of the Survey on Household Budgets. Enquete nationale sur le budget, la consommation et le niveau de vie des ménages–2000. Volume A. Resultats de l'Enquete sur le Budget des ménages,* p. 33.

UNDP (United Nations Development Programme). 2003. *Human Development Report: Millennium Development Goals—A Compact among Nations to End Human Poverty.* New York, NY: Oxford University Press.

World Bank. 2004. *Doing Business in 2004: Understanding Regulation.* Washington, D.C.: World Bank and Oxford University Press. Doing Business Database available at http://rru.worldbank.org/DoingBusiness.

———. 2003a. *Tunisia: Project Performance Assessment Report,* Agricultural Research and Extension Project (Loan No. 3217), Agricultural Sector Investment Project (Loan No. 3661), Northwest Mountainous Areas Development Project (Loan No. 3691), National Rural Finance Project (Loan No. 3892), Report No. 26260, June 26, 2003. Washington D.C.

———. 2003b. *Jobs, Growth, and Governance in the Middle East and North Africa: Unlocking the Potential for Prosperity.* Washington, D.C.: World Bank.

———. 2002. "Jordan—Development Policy Review: A Reforming State in a Volatile Region." Report No. 24425. Washington, D.C.

———. 2000a. *Republic of Tunisia: Private Sector Assessment Update—Meeting the Challenge of Globalization.* 3 vols. Report No. 20173-TUN. Washington, D.C.

———. 2000b. *Republic of Tunisia: Social and Structural Review 2000—Integrating into the World Economy and Sustaining Economic and Social Progress.* Report No. 20976. Washington, D.C.

———. 2000c. "Tunisia—Country Assistance Strategy."

————. 1995a. *Republic of Tunisia: Towards the 21st Century*. Country Economic Memorandum Report No. 14375-TUN. Washington, D.C.

————. 1995b. *Tunisia: Poverty Alleviation*. Report No. 13993. Washington, D.C.

————. 1994a. *Kingdom of Morocco, Republic of Tunisia—Export Growth: Determinants and Prospects*. Report No. 12947. Washington, D.C.

————. 1994b. *Republic of Tunisia: Private Sector Assessment*. Report No. 12945-TUN. Washington, D.C.